CAREC GENDER ASSESSMENT

SUPPLEMENTARY DOCUMENT FOR THE CAREC GENDER STRATEGY 2030

JANUARY 2021

Notes:
In this publication, "$" refers to United States dollars.
ADB recognizes "China" as the People's Republic of China.

On the cover: Women and girls in CAREC member countries (photos by ADB Photo Library).

Cover design by Jasper Lauzon.

CONTENTS

TABLES, FIGURES, AND BOXES

ABBREVIATIONS

ACTED	Agency for Technical Cooperation and Development
ADB	Asian Development Bank
BWA	business women association(s)
CAREC	Central Asia Regional Economic Cooperation
EBRD	European Bank for Reconstruction and Development
EGM	effective gender mainstreaming
FAO	Food and Agriculture Organization of the United Nations
GDI	Gender Development Index
GDP	gross domestic product
GEF	Global Environment Facility
GEN	gender equity
GGGI	Global Gender Gap Index
GII	Gender Inequality Index
ICT	information and communication technology
MMR	maternal mortality ratio
MSMEs	micro, small, and medium-sized enterprises
NGE	no gender elements
PPTA	project preparatory technical assistance
PRC	People's Republic of China
SDG	Sustainable Development Goal
SGE	some gender elements
STEM	science, technology, engineering, and mathematics
TVET	technical and vocational education and training
UNDP	United Nations Development Programme
WEF	World Economic Forum

EXECUTIVE SUMMARY

I. INTRODUCTION

The Central Asia Regional Economic Cooperation (CAREC) Program is a regional partnership of 11 countries—Afghanistan, Azerbaijan, the People's Republic of China (PRC), Georgia, Kazakhstan, the Kyrgyz Republic, Mongolia, Pakistan, Tajikistan, Turkmenistan, and Uzbekistan—and development partners who work together to promote development through cooperation, leading to accelerated economic growth and poverty reduction.

The program is guided by the CAREC 2030 strategy, endorsed in 2017, which states that more attention will be paid to gender equality as a cross-cutting issue over the five envisioned operational clusters: (i) economic and financial stability; (ii) trade, tourism, and economic corridors; (iii) infrastructure and economic connectivity; (iv) agriculture and water; and (v) human development. Integrating the effective use of information and communication technology (ICT) in CAREC operations is a cross-cutting priority. The challenge of implementing the CAREC 2030 strategy in a gender-responsive and gender-sensitive manner shows the need for a regional approach grounded in evidence from across member countries to better align gender activities. Seeking such alignment is consistent with CAREC countries' commitment to advancing gender equality and women's and girls' empowerment to help achieve increased economic growth, inclusive social development, and the Sustainable Development Goals.

This assessment provides a diagnostic framework to analyze the level of gender equality in CAREC countries and to assess the CAREC Program's performance in gender mainstreaming in its operations for the period from 2001 to 2018. A mixed-methods approach was adopted for the assessment, involving a desk review supplemented by country visits to Azerbaijan, Kazakhstan, and Uzbekistan.

II. GENDER EQUALITY IN CAREC COUNTRIES: PROGRESS AND GAPS

A. Key Gender Global Indicators for CAREC Countries

Most of the CAREC countries have national legislation to promote gender equality and prohibit gender-based discrimination. However, national statistics and global gender indicators point to persistent gender-based disparities in all CAREC countries, these being particularly acute in economic empowerment and political representation.

According to the 2018 Gender Inequality Index from the United Nations Development Programme (UNDP), all CAREC countries, with the exception of the PRC and Kazakhstan, which ranked 39th and 46th, respectively, fall into the lowest two-thirds of the ranked 189 countries.

The 2018 Gender Development Index from UNDP rates all CAREC countries as having very high, high, or medium human development, except for Afghanistan, which is rated at low human development.

The 2020 Global Gender Gap Index from the World Economic Forum ranks Kazakhstan at 72nd and Georgia at 74th out of 153 countries, while Pakistan scores the lowest among the CAREC countries at 151st.

Finally, data extracted from gender parity measures from the McKinsey Global Institute indicate that even the countries with the best rankings, such as the PRC and Kazakhstan, still have room for improvement before achieving gender parity in access for women to work and essential services.

B. Cross-Cutting Gender and Human Development Issues

In addition to the gender disparities in CAREC countries demonstrated by the global gender indicators, the limited participation of women in the following seven areas is further analyzed as a cause for those disparities. These continue to undermine the potential for achieving gender equality as envisioned in the Sustainable Development Goals.

1.   Women's Access to Decent Work

- **Low economic participation of women.** There is lower participation of women than men in the labor market in all 11 CAREC member countries. There is a particularly wide gap in Pakistan, where only 24% of employment-age women participate in the labor market compared with 81.5% of men, followed by Tajikistan and Afghanistan, where around 50% fewer women than men participate in the formal labor market. Evidence shows that fast economic growth does not automatically reduce gender inequality. However, it is estimated that women's higher participation in the labor force can help increase the gross domestic product of global and national economies up to 60%, in the case of Pakistan between 2014 and 2025, for example.

- **Significant gender wage gap.** Women in CAREC countries are concentrated in lower-paid sectors such as agriculture, education, health care, and hospitality, whereas men predominate in well-paid sectors such as finance, engineering, and transport. Women also face gender-based inequalities in the form of gender biases in hiring practices and promotion opportunities; failures to implement national policies on paid maternity and paternity leave, flexible working arrangements, and equal pay; and sexual harassment in the workplace.

- **Disproportionate unpaid care work by women.** Measures such as subsidized childcare and flexible working hours are limited, which affects women's economic participation in many CAREC countries. For example, in Kazakhstan, women spend around 17.1% of their time in unpaid care work in addition to undertaking paid work, compared to men, who devote only around 7.1% of their time to unpaid care work.

- **Overrepresentation of women in the informal sector.** Work in the informal sector lacks in security and social protection, involves hard labor, is low paying, and provides limited opportunities for human capital development. Although data are not available for all CAREC countries, data from Afghanistan, Azerbaijan, Mongolia, and Pakistan report a high proportion of women as unpaid family workers.

2.   Women's Access to Economic Opportunities

- **Entrepreneurship.** Women also find social and financial difficulties in setting up and running a business, including limited access to finance, limited business capacity, undermined support due to gender norms, competing demands of unpaid care work, lack of income security and access to social protection benefits, and lack of networking.

For example, in the Kyrgyz Republic in 2017, loans for female borrowers accounted for only 25%–43% of banks' total loan portfolio. The percentage of women entrepreneurs in Uzbekistan is high, with 42% of micro, small, and medium-sized enterprises being run by women.

- **Border trade.** Women are often involved in formal and informal cross-border trading activities. They tend to travel by foot, which is time-consuming and unsafe. They are also less informed about market rules, which makes them more likely to become targets of harassment and extortion. Removing barriers and including women in supply chains can propel growth in the region.

- **Tourism.** In CAREC countries, women are engaged directly in the tourism industry in services such as handicraft production, catering, and guesthouses. There is great potential to increase women's business and employment in the sector, but it is vital to minimize any risks of sexual harassment, exploitation, and human trafficking, which affect women disproportionately.

- **Agriculture.** Male labor migration in the last 2 decades has driven women's increased participation in the agriculture sector. The agricultural share of economically active women substantially varies among CAREC countries. In Afghanistan, 82% of the economically active women work in agriculture, followed by 64% in the PRC; this percentage is only 6.8% for Kazakhstan and 11.7% for Georgia. This work is often unpaid or poorly paid, and women farmers face challenges that include limited access to productive resources such as land and water, and to strategic assets such as market linkages and information, finance, and value chains.

3.   Women's Participation in Decision-Making

In all CAREC countries, women have the right to participate in public life and hold public office, yet in all 11 countries, women's political participation falls well below the 33% advocated by the Beijing Platform for Action. Evidence also indicates that the number of women in managerial positions in CAREC countries is still low in both public sector institutions and private sector companies. For example, in 2017, Mongolia had the highest rate of women in managerial positions (40.8%), followed by the Kyrgyz Republic (36.2%) and Azerbaijan (34.5%), while Pakistan had only 2.9%.

4.   Women's and Girls' Access to Education and Training

Gender parity or near parity has been achieved in education in most CAREC countries, measured in terms of the percentage of the population with at least some secondary education. While there is reverse gender gap in Mongolia and Tajikistan, where more girls than boys receive secondary education, in Afghanistan only 13.2% of girls attended secondary school in 2018. Despite the growing number of women with secondary and tertiary education in many CAREC countries, female student participation is still low in science, technology, engineering, and mathematics (STEM) courses. The choice of courses for female students is strongly influenced by gender norms and perceptions.

5.   Women's and Girls' Access to Health Services

There has been a steady improvement in health care provision in most CAREC countries, but access continues to be poor in some countries, and this is reflected in a relatively high maternal mortality ratio. While the ratio has slightly decreased or remained steady during the last years, Afghanistan has the highest maternal mortality ratio of all CAREC countries, with 638 maternal deaths out of 100,000 live births registered in 2017, followed by Pakistan with 140; these can be compared with Turkmenistan, where the ratio decreased to 7 in the same year, and Kazakhstan with 10.

6.   Women's and Girls' Access to Information and Communication Technology

Across all 11 CAREC countries, women have less access than men to ICT. Evidence shows that in 2019, 90% of women in Central Asia owned mobile phones, while 17 million women remained unconnected. In the PRC, there is near gender parity in mobile internet usage (82% of men and 81% of women). The gender gap for Pakistan is the widest with only 11% of women and 38% of men being mobile internet users.

7.   Women's Access to Infrastructure and Public Services

- **Transport.** There are significant gender differences in trip patterns and mobility constraints in CAREC countries, resulting in gender differences in the purpose of travel and mode of transport used. On average, women make fewer and shorter daily trips than men, are less likely to drive and own a vehicle than men, and are more likely to travel by foot. Women are also more likely than men to use public transport, where sexual harassment is a growing problem in some CAREC countries. Women's lack of access to safe public transport hinders their access to work and negatively affects school attendance for female students. The transport sector is a potential source of employment for women but in many CAREC countries women are less likely to apply for these positions because they often lack technical training.

- **Energy.** In some CAREC countries, households have electricity for only 3 to 7 hours per day during the winter, so they often need to supplement their energy with solid and fossil fuels. This disproportionately affects women and girls, as it often falls to them to collect fuel or prepare stoves for cooking and heating, resulting in time poverty and exposure to sexual harassment. Women's and children's health is also more likely to be negatively affected by poor air quality in homes due to burning biofuels. The energy sector could provide a useful source of employment for women, particularly in the rapidly expanding sustainable energy market. However, available data indicate that in many CAREC countries, technical occupations in sectors such as energy are currently dominated by men.

- **Water.** In CAREC countries, women often have the primary responsibility for water management for the household and are, therefore, disproportionately burdened by water supply and quality issues. Outdated infrastructure and inadequate water supply place additional burdens on women. Access to a modern, reliable water supply can, therefore, vastly improve the quality of life of women and their families.

III. GENDER INCLUSION ANALYSIS OF CAREC PROJECTS

A selection of 107 CAREC projects implemented between 2014 and 2018 were analyzed to identify good practices, gaps, and missed opportunities in gender mainstreaming. This sample includes country-specific and regional projects implemented in all 11 CAREC countries, through loans and technical assistance, by different CAREC development partners. The full list of projects reviewed can be found in Appendix 1. As the majority of these initiatives (91 out of 107) are Asian Development Bank (ADB) projects, the assessment refers to ADB's system of categories classifying projects according to the degree to which gender elements are included: gender equity (GEN), effective gender mainstreaming (EGM), some gender elements (SGE), and no gender elements (NGE). The other donors involved in these projects include the European Bank for Reconstruction and Development, Global Environment Facility, the Islamic Development Bank, UNDP, and the World Bank.

■ **Transport project analysis.** Of the 64 ADB-funded reviewed projects on transport, 29 are classified as EGM or SGE and none are classified GEN. Seven projects funded by other organizations also contain gender elements. For some of the projects classified as SGE, the gender-responsive features are nonexistent or minimal. However, there are multiple examples of good or emerging good practices. These gender-inclusive features include HIV prevention and anti-human-trafficking measures; the installation of overpasses, bridges, and zebra crossings on busy roads and separate toilet facilities for men and women along major routes; ensuring equal opportunities and equal pay for women and men for positions in CAREC-funded sectors; provision of on-the-job skills building and training in CAREC projects; and the establishment of quotas and minimum numbers for hiring women in CAREC-funded projects.

■ **Energy project analysis.** A total of 26 energy projects were reviewed. Of the 16 ADB-funded projects, 10 are classified as NGE. Six projects are classified as being SGE or EGM but only two have any gender design features. Gender-responsive project design features include quotas for the inclusion of women in consultation processes during planning and implementation phases; efforts to promote women's economic empowerment and capacity through the increased recruitment of female staff, including in technical areas such as engineering and through training of female entrepreneurs in green energy supply; and educating women on the safe use of labor and energy-saving electrical and gas-powered devices in the home.

■ **Trade project analysis.** Of the 11 trade-related projects reviewed, only one was categorized as SGE. The remaining 10 projects were all categorized as NGE and there were no projects from funders other than ADB. The gender-related activities of the SGE project Mongolia: Regional Improvement of Border Services Project included the establishment of a threshold for female employment in the project, and training of customs and border staff on sexually transmitted infections and human trafficking.

IV. MAINSTREAMING GENDER IN CAREC OPERATIONS: ENTRY POINTS

Both the analysis of women's situation in CAREC countries and the reviewed CAREC projects show that there are promising good practices emerging in addressing women's concerns and increasing their economic participation. However, there is considerable room to improve, scale up, and mainstream gender across the whole range of CAREC operations at both cross-cutting and sector-specific levels.

Cross-cutting recommendations include (i) conducting comprehensive social inclusion assessments from the outset of any project, (ii) developing a regional gender action plan, and (iii) setting minimum gender equality and inclusion standards.

The following sector-specific recommendations may guide the formulation of strategic directions and entry points under the CAREC 2030 gender strategy. These recommendations are grouped for the five CAREC operational clusters, plus an additional area for gender mainstreaming into ICT.

A. Economic and Financial Stability

Strategic directions for mainstreaming gender into this cluster include generating economic opportunities for women through policies and strategies. These include setting targets for the employment of women—including in nontraditional jobs and management—and creating employment standards that promote decent work for all. These also mean creating an enabling environment for female entrepreneurs, including the promotion of improved financial access, and building women's and girls' capacity in STEM subjects and ICT. Measures are also needed to promote policy dialogue at regional and cross-country levels. Gender-responsive adjustments in the banking sector are also required, including better coordinated banking regulations to improve financial inclusion for women, supported by regional financial models that promote female entrepreneurship.

B. Trade, Tourism, and Economic Corridors

- **Trade.** National and regional trade policies should be revised to introduce gender-responsive measures, including finance policies promoting women-owned micro, small, and medium-sized enterprises and policies that create an enabling environment for the economic empowerment of female entrepreneurs and informal cross-border traders. These policies should be informed through consultations with female traders and entrepreneurs. Information and appropriate training should be provided for police, border staff, and customs officials to reduce the risk of human trafficking, sexual exploitation, gender-based violence, and sexual harassment.

- **Tourism.** Equal access to information about tourism-related jobs should be promoted. Local communities should be involved in the planning and development of regional tourism plans to ensure they will directly benefit from these initiatives. Targeted information and training in avoiding human trafficking and sexual exploitation should be promoted.

- **Economic corridors.** Economic corridors offer opportunities for job creation and the promotion of entrepreneurship. The Almaty-Bishkek Economic Corridor and the Trilateral Economic Corridor connecting Kazakhstan, Uzbekistan, and Tajikistan could be used to increase women's participation in all related activities such as cross-border trade, tourism and related services, regional value chains, urban planning, and knowledge-sharing and training events.

C. Infrastructure and Connectivity

- **Transport.** It is vital to ensure regional coordination in setting standards for design features of transport-related infrastructure and services across CAREC countries and corridors. Adequate lighting must be provided along routes to bus stops and local villages. Suitable walkways, pedestrian bridges, and bus shelters must be provided to ensure accessibility, comfort, and safety. Accessible gender-sensitive amenities must be provided for both women and men on major transport routes. To reduce the risk of sexual and other forms of harassment for women using public transport, measures such as training in protecting women for transport service providers, the introduction of zero-tolerance policies for any form of sexual harassment, and raising public awareness of these issues could be implemented. Regional and national-level policies and guidelines should be established to increase employment opportunities for women in transport, going beyond roles in administration and encouraging their application for technical and managerial roles.

■ **Energy.** All aspects of energy projects and service designs should be grounded in gender-sensitive evidence gathered through consultative processes and surveys to grant access to affordable, safe, and modern energy. National and regional information systems should be created or improved to generate sex-disaggregated data on issues such as accessibility, affordability, and income generation to inform energy planning. Economic opportunities should be created for women in the emerging green energy sector through specific trainings.

D. Agriculture and Water

Development of both regional and country-level approaches to promote equal ownership and access to land, credit, and digital technologies is necessary to reduce the agriculture sector gender gap in CAREC countries. Regional agricultural value chain channels should be strengthened, including through promoting participation of female producers, supported by the development of digital platforms to promote gender-sensitive cross-border agricultural trade. Consultation with female beneficiaries should be sought in the design process. Active recruitment of women for technical and managerial roles in the water sector and the provision of on-the-job training should also be promoted. Regional mechanisms for transboundary water resource management should be designed, and women's participation in these mechanisms should be ensured.

E. Human Development Cluster

■ **Education.** CAREC should actively promote better alignment of women's educational choices with employment opportunities nationally and across the CAREC region. Strategies at regional and intercountry levels could include partnering with national and regional technical and vocational education and training providers to offer courses for women in STEM subjects. Steps should also be taken to increase women's representation in management positions in education.

■ **Health.** A regional approach to strengthen surveillance systems and monitoring capabilities across borders for the control of communicable and noncommunicable diseases and to improve access of women and men to quality and more affordable services should be pursued. Knowledge sharing on new technologies for maternal health care and the provision of services to remote, underserved areas should be encouraged.

F. Information and Communication Technology

CAREC can help close the digital gender divide by supporting capacity building in ICT for women and girls of all ages in urban and rural areas. Partnerships with private sector digital providers to support the provision of internet access to poor households and women entrepreneur's use of digital platforms could also be promoted. Regional networks to share gender-sensitive practices for enhancing women's access to ICT and increasing their opportunities in information technology–related employment could also be established.

## CHAPTER I

INTRODUCTION

A. Background of CAREC and the 2030 Strategy

1. In 2017, the 16th Central Asia Regional Economic Cooperation (CAREC) Ministerial Conference endorsed CAREC's new long-term strategy, CAREC 2030: Connecting the Region for Shared and Sustainable Development. It is guided by the overarching vision of "Good neighbors, good partners, and good prospects" to create an "open and inclusive platform for regional cooperation to connect people, policies and projects for shared and sustainable development."

2. The strategy states that more attention will be paid to gender equality as a cross-cutting issue and consequently its vision should be implemented in a gender-responsive and gender-sensitive manner. Planning and implementation of the CAREC 2030 strategy must take into account the specific needs of women, men, and children and contribute to gender equality and women's empowerment in the region. In addition, there is consensus among CAREC member countries and development partners on the importance of gender mainstreaming in CAREC to help achieve increased economic growth, inclusive social development, and the Sustainable Development Goals (SDGs).

3. This shows the need for a regional strategic approach grounded in evidence from across CAREC countries to better align gender activities among member countries and across CAREC operational clusters to achieve common objectives.[1] However, country-level initiatives must also respond to particular gender-related challenges and opportunities.

B. Purpose and Scope of Work

4. This CAREC gender assessment has been developed with the purpose of serving as a diagnostic framework to analyze the gender situation in the 11 CAREC countries[2] and to evaluate how CAREC has been mainstreaming gender across the three sectors of transport, energy, and trade, which were priority sectors from the inception of CAREC in 2001 through 2018. The data, examples, and findings of this assessment serve as the base and major inputs for the CAREC Gender Strategy 2030 and for the identification of gender entry points for future planning.

5. For the sectoral gender evaluation, a total of 107 projects implemented by CAREC and development partners during 2014–2018 were reviewed. This selection includes national and regional projects, with representation of all 11 CAREC countries on transport, trade, energy, or multisector projects, including loans and technical assistance. The gender evaluation enables conclusions to be drawn about gaps, missed opportunities, and ultimately entry points

---

[1] Operational priorities under CAREC 2030 fall into five clusters: (i) economic and financial stability; (ii) trade, tourism, and economic corridors; (iii) infrastructure and connectivity; (iv) agriculture and water; and (v) human development, while gender equality, information and communication technology (ICT), and climate change are cross-cutting priorities in CAREC operations.

[2] The CAREC member countries are Afghanistan, Azerbaijan, the People's Republic of China (PRC), Georgia, Kazakhstan, the Kyrgyz Republic, Mongolia, Pakistan, Tajikistan, Turkmenistan, and Uzbekistan.

for the five CAREC operational clusters. Appendix 1 provides a full list of reviewed projects and Appendix 2 lists the reviewed projects for the transport sector, as they were too numerous for the main text.

C. Structure of the CAREC Gender Assessment

6.   The assessment has four main chapters. After the introduction, Chapter 2 provides a situational gender analysis of key gender issues and sectors for CAREC countries, outlines the progress of the countries in light of key global gender indicators, and then moves to a deeper analysis, drawing on evidence from across CAREC countries to inform understanding of gender dimensions across seven focal areas.

7.   Chapter 3 investigates and analyzes a selection of 107 projects implemented by CAREC and development partners, with a focus on good practices, gaps, and opportunities for mainstreaming gender.

8.   Finally, Chapter 4 summarizes potential gender entry points for all CAREC clusters, which have served as a base to formulate the strategic guidelines and entry points of the CAREC Gender Strategy 2030. A full detailed list of entry points can be found in Appendix 1 of the strategy.

D. Methodology for the CAREC Gender Assessment

9.   A mixed-methods approach was adopted for the assessment, involving a desk review supplemented by country visits to Azerbaijan, Kazakhstan, and Uzbekistan.[3] Key stakeholders engaged for discussion during the country missions included professional business women associations and civil society organizations, ADB staff members responsible for CAREC projects, program coordinators, advisors to national focal points, and other development partners.

---

[3]   See Appendix 3: Key Findings from Country Research Missions to Azerbaijan, Kazakhstan, and Uzbekistan.

## CHAPTER II

GENDER EQUALITY IN CAREC COUNTRIES: PROGRESS AND GAPS

10.   This chapter assesses progress and gaps with regard to gender equality and women's empowerment in areas of particular relevance for CAREC 2030 and CAREC countries. Section A provides an overview of key global gender indicators for CAREC countries, while section B considers cross-cutting gender and human development issues in detail, grounded in data from global databases and in-country evidence, with a focus on seven key areas.

A. Key Gender Indicators for CAREC Countries

11.   The global indicators outlined in this section provide a very general overall picture of gender inequalities in CAREC countries and reflect some broad similarities such as the gender gap in accessing decent employment and political representation. They also reveal significant differences between countries and the value of gaining a more detailed understanding of these specificities.

12.   In the majority of CAREC countries, national legislation exists to promote gender equality and nondiscrimination. However, national statistics and global gender indicators gathered by the United Nations Development Programme (UNDP), the World Economic Forum (WEF), and the McKinsey Global Institute point to persistent gender-based disparities across multiple indices in all CAREC countries.

1.   United Nations Development Programme's Gender Inequality Index

13.   The Gender Inequality Index (GII) provides a composite score based on gender parity in education and labor markets, maternal and adolescent mortality rates, and women's parliamentary representation.[4] According to the 2018 GII, all CAREC countries, with the exception of the People's Republic of China (PRC) and Kazakhstan, fall into the lowest two-thirds of 189 countries (Table 1). This indicator shows stark divergences among CAREC countries in the ways gender disparities manifest.

14.   **Maternal mortality ratio.** The maternal mortality ratio (MMR) in Afghanistan registered 638 maternal deaths out of 100,000 live births registered in 2017, followed by Pakistan with 140; this can be compared with Turkmenistan, where the ratio decreases to 7 in the same year, and Kazakhstan with 10.[5]

---

[4]   UNDP. 2020. *Gender Inequality Index*. http://hdr.undp.org/en/content/gender-inequality-index-gii (accessed 2 March 2020).

[5]   UNICEF Data. 2019. *Trends in Estimates of Maternal Mortality Ratio (MMR), Maternal Deaths and Lifetime Risk of Maternal Death, 2000–2017*. https://data.unicef.org/resources/dataset/maternal-mortality-data/ (accessed October 2020).

Table 1: Consolidated View of United Nations Development Programme and World Economic Forum Gender Indicators

Country	UNDP GII 2018		UNDP GDI 2018		WEF GGGI 2020	
	Rank	Score	Rank[a]	Score	Rank	Score
Afghanistan	143	0.575	N/A	0.496	N/A	N/A
Azerbaijan	70	0.321	N/A	0.754	94	0.687
People's Republic of China	39	0.163	N/A	0.758	106	0.676
Georgia	75	0.351	N/A	0.786	74	0.708
Kazakhstan	46	0.203	N/A	0.999	72	0.710
Kyrgyz Republic	87	0381	N/A	0.674	93	0.689
Mongolia	71	0.322	N/A	1.023	79	0.706
Pakistan	136	0.547	N/A	0.560	151	0.564
Tajikistan	84	0.377	N/A	0.656	137	0.626
Turkmenistan[b]	N/A	N/A	N/A	N/A	N/A	N/A
Uzbekistan	64	0.303	N/A	0.710	N/A	N/A

GII = Gender Inequality Index, GDI = Gender Development Index, GGGI = Global Gender Gap Index, N/A = not applicable, UNDP = United Nations Development Programme, WEF = World Economic Forum.

[a] There is no rank available for the UNDP GDI.

[b] No overall score or ranking is available for Turkmenistan but there are available figures on material mortality ratio and women's and men's economic participation.

Sources: UNDP Gender Inequality Index, 2018; UNDP Gender Development Index, 2018; WEF Global Gender Gap Index, 2020.

15. **Representation in Parliament.** Although all countries fall below the Beijing Platform for Action target of 30% women's representation in Parliament, there are significant regional disparities in this regard.[6] In Afghanistan, 27.4% of seats were held by women in 2018 while in the PRC, the figure was 24.9% and in Turkmenistan, 24.8%. However, in Georgia, Uzbekistan, and Mongolia, women accounted for only 16.0%, 16.4%, and 17.1% of parliamentarians, respectively, in the same period.

16. However, there are also clear commonalities. The GII reveals a systemic gender gap in labor force participation across most CAREC countries, with disparities in employment rates, pay scales, and quality of employment.

17. **Participation in labor market.** Economic participation of women is relatively low compared with men in all CAREC countries, with a particularly wide gap in Pakistan, where only 23.9% of employment-age women participate in the labor market compared with 81.5% of men, followed by Tajikistan and Afghanistan, where around 50% fewer women than men participate in the formal labor market. By contrast, Azerbaijan achieves near gender parity in labor participation (at 63.1% to 69.7%) but the figures reflect a national employment deficit for both women and men.

---

[6] The Beijing Declaration and Platform for Action was endorsed at the 4th World Conference on Women of the UN in Beijing, PRC in 1995. It is considered the most comprehensive global policy framework for the rights of women. It recognizes women's rights as human rights and lays out a road map for achieving gender equality, including specific measures and outcomes across issues affecting women and girls (The Beijing Platform for Action: inspiration then and now | UN Women – Beijing+20).

18. **Education.** In the majority of CAREC countries, gender parity or near parity has been achieved in education, measured in terms of the percentage of the population with at least some secondary education. However, in Tajikistan and Mongolia, there is a reverse gender gap with a substantially higher percentage of girls than boys receiving secondary education (98.8% of girls compared with 87.0% of boys in Tajikistan and 91.3% of girls compared with 86.3% of boys in Mongolia). In Pakistan and Afghanistan, overall rates of secondary education are low, but there is a significant gender gap with only 26.7% of girls in Pakistan attending secondary school compared with 47.3% of boys. The gap is the starkest in Afghanistan, where only 13.2% of females were recorded as having achieved some secondary education in 2018, compared with 36.9% of males.

2. United Nations Development Programme's Gender Development Index

19. The Gender Development Index (GDI) "measures gender gaps in human development achievements by accounting for disparities between women and men in three basic dimensions of human development—health, knowledge, and living standards—using the same component indicators as in the Human Development Index" (Table 1).[7]

20. Kazakhstan is rated very high in terms of human development; Azerbaijan, the PRC, Georgia, Mongolia, Turkmenistan, and Uzbekistan are ranked high in human development; the Kyrgyz Republic, Tajikistan, and Pakistan are ranked medium in human development; and Afghanistan is ranked low in human development.

3. World Economic Forum's Global Gender Gap Index

21. The Global Gender Gap Index (GGGI) measures gender-based gaps in access to resources and opportunities based on four categories: (i) economic participation and opportunity, (ii) educational attainment, (iii) health and survival, and (iv) political empowerment.

22. The most recent GGGI index (Table 1) includes data on 153 countries, including eight CAREC countries, namely Azerbaijan, the PRC, Georgia, Kazakhstan, the Kyrgyz Republic, Mongolia, Tajikistan, and Pakistan.[8] Of these countries, Kazakhstan and Georgia lead among CAREC countries, ranked at 72nd and 74th, respectively. Tajikistan is in the next lowest overall of the CAREC countries, ranked at 137th. Pakistan scores the lowest of CAREC countries in the GGGI and is near the bottom of all countries ranked at 151st, with only Iraq and Yemen below it at 152nd and 153rd, respectively.

23. **Educational parity.** On specific indicators under the GGGI, most CAREC countries fare reasonably well in terms of educational parity, with only Pakistan scoring below 0.900, at 0.823.

24. **Economic participation.** There is a wide disparity in ranking for the economic participation indicator. Only Kazakhstan, Azerbaijan, and Mongolia are ranked in the top third, with Mongolia ranking 29th (and scoring 0.751), Azerbaijan ranking 33rd (and scoring 0.748), and Kazakhstan ranking 37th (with a score of 0.742). At the other end of the scale, Pakistan is ranked 150th for women's economic participation and scores only 0.327. Tajikistan also scores poorly, ranking 134th on this indicator.

---

[7] UNDP. 2020. *Gender Development Index*. http://hdr.undp.org/en/content/gender-development-index-gdi.

[8] World Economic Forum. 2020. *Global Gender Gap Report*. Washington, DC: WEF. http://www3.weforum.org/docs/WEF_GGGR_2020.pdf.

25.   **Political participation.** No countries ranked highly on women's political participation, but Pakistan, Georgia, and the PRC are ranked in the top two-thirds, at 93rd, 94th, and 95th, respectively. By contrast, Azerbaijan scores poorly on women's political representation, ranking 140th, followed by Tajikistan (at 128th) and Mongolia (at 120th).

4.   McKinsey Global Institute's Gender Parity Measures

26.   The McKinsey Global Institute has measured levels of gender parity in certain CAREC countries, using a combined indicator of access to both decent work and essential services (Table 2). "Work parity" is measured by comparing women's and men's ability to find a job and obtain a fair compensation for it. It also compares women's and men's ability to equitably share unpaid care work and occupy leadership positions with high performance. "Essential services" is measured by comparing women's and men's access to services that are critical for economic participation, such as health, education, financial, and technology-related services. The "gender parity" score is an aggregate measure of how close women are to gender parity in any given country. A score of 100 indicates complete parity. A gender parity score of 40, for example, indicates that on average women have only 40% of the opportunities that men do, measured in terms of 15 selected indicators.

27.   These figures reflect, to an extent, the disparities among CAREC countries in terms of gender parity, but indicate that even the countries with the best rank, such as the PRC and Kazakhstan, have some way to go before achieving parity in access to decent work for women.

Table 2: **Gender Parity in Selected CAREC Countries**

Country[a]	Gender Parity	
	Access to Decent Work	**Access to Essential Services**
Azerbaijan	68	81
People's Republic of China	69	93
Kazakhstan	69	92
Pakistan	48	55
Uzbekistan	62	74

[a]   The report from which these figures are taken only provides data and projections for the five CAREC countries shown here.

Source: McKinsey Global Institute. 2015. *The Power of Parity: How Advancing Women's Equality Can Add $12 Trillion to Global Growth.* https://www.mckinsey.com/~/media/McKinsey/Industries/Public%20and%20Social%20Sector/Our%20Insights/How%20advancing%20womens%20equality%20can%20add%2012%20trillion%20to%20global%20growth/MGI%20Power%20of%20parity_Full%20report_September%202015.pdf.

B. Cross-Cutting Gender and Human Development Issues

28.   This section provides further analysis of these gender disparities, with a focus on seven specific areas: (i) women's access to decent work, (ii) women's access to economic opportunities, (iii) women's participation in decision-making, (iv) women's and girls' access to education and training, (v) women's and girls' access to health services, (vi) women and girls' access to information and communication technology (ICT), and (vii) women's access to infrastructure and public services.

29.   These areas, which are highlighted under the SDGs, continue to seriously undermine the potential for achieving equal rights, opportunities, and quality of life for women not only in CAREC countries but also in many other parts of the world. As well as being a vital goal in its own right, SDG 5 is a cross-cutting goal for all SDGs in recognition that economic and social development are contingent on the achievement of gender equality.

30.   The section also points to some of the causes behind the divergences in indicators among CAREC countries.

1.   Women's Access to Decent Work

31.   **Economic policies affect women differently.** Macroeconomic policy is often considered gender neutral, benefiting both women and men equally. However, economic policies and fiscal measures often affect women and men very differently. Evidence shows that fast economic growth does not automatically reduce gender inequality.[9] The International Monetary Fund (IMF) recognizes that, despite progress achieved in addressing gender inequalities, disparities between women and men persist on a global scale: "Women and men do not have the same opportunities to participate in economic activity, and when women do participate, they do not receive the same recognition, wages, or benefits as men."[10]

32.   **Economic gains from women's participation in the labor force.** It is estimated that if women in Europe and Central Asia alone were able to participate equally in the labor force, they would contribute as much as $1.1 trillion to the global economy. Women in South Asia, excluding India, would provide an additional $500 billion.[11] Women's participation in the labor force can also contribute to the gross domestic product (GDP) of national economies, thereby helping to improve the well-being of all citizens. The economic gains that are possible in selected CAREC countries are shown in Table 3.

---

[9]   See Gender and Development Network. 2016. Breaking Down the Barriers: Macroeconomic Policies that Promote Women's Economic Equality. *GADN Briefing*. https://gadnetwork.org/gadn-resources/2016/7/7/breaking-down-the-barriers-macroeconomic-policies-that-promote-womens-economic-equality. See also McKinsey Global Institute. 2015. *The Power of Parity: How Advancing Women's Equality Can Add $12 Trillion to Global Growth*. https://www.mckinsey.com/~/media/McKinsey/Industries/Public%20and%20Social%20Sector/Our%20Insights/How%20advancing%20womens%20equality%20can%20add%2012%20trillion%20to%20global%20growth/MGI%20Power%20of%20parity_Full%20report_September%202015.pdf.

[10]   IMF. 2018. *Pursuing Women's Economic Empowerment*. Background Note for the Meeting of G7 Ministers and Central Bank Governors, June 2018. *IMF Policy Papers*. https://www.imf.org/en/Publications/Policy-Papers/Issues/2018/05/31/pp053118pursuing-womens-economic-empowerment.

[11]   McKinsey Global Institute. 2015. The Power of Parity: How Advancing Women's Equality Can Add $12 Trillion to Global Growth. https://www.mckinsey.com/~/media/McKinsey/Industries/Public%20and%20Social%20Sector/Our%20Insights/How%20advancing%20womens%20equality%20can%20add%2012%20trillion%20to%20global%20growth/MGI%20Power%20of%20parity_Full%20report_September%202015.pdf.

Table 3: Economic Gains of Female Labor Force Participation in Selected Countries

Country[a]	GDP Increase (2014–2025)		
	GDP Increase (%)	GDP Increase ($)	Per Capita Increase ($)
Azerbaijan	24	27 billion	2,785
People's Republic of China	20	4.2 trillion	2,990
Kazakhstan	16	53 billion	2,997
Pakistan	60	251 billion	1,324
Uzbekistan	36	33 billion	1,070

GDP = gross domestic product.

[a]   The report from which these figures are taken only provides data and projections for the five CAREC countries shown.

Source: McKinsey Global Institute. 2015. *The Power of Parity: How Advancing Women's Equality Can Add $12 Trillion to Global Growth.* https://www.mckinsey.com/~/media/McKinsey/Industries/Public%20and%20Social%20Sector/Our%20Insights/How%20advancing%20womens%20equality%20can%20add%2012%20trillion%20to%20global%20growth/ MGI%20Power%20of%20parity_Full%20report_September%202015.pdf.

33.   **Limited opportunities for women.** The range and quality of available opportunities are limited for women in CAREC countries. Not only do relatively fewer women work, but those who do work pursue different occupations than men, are paid less, and work fewer hours. This is mostly a function of historical and structural variables, such as normative gender roles and the lack of market and industry adaptation to a more diverse workforce, but ongoing discrimination against women is also a factor in creating this disparity.

34.   **Disparities in women's access to decent work.** The gender disparities in access to decent work in CAREC countries are reflected in the GII and GGGI indicators for 2020, which reveal lower participation of women than men in the labor market in all 11 countries, with the widest gaps in Afghanistan, Pakistan, and Tajikistan. In some countries, the gender ratio for employment has been widening. In Pakistan, the ratio of employed females over 15 years doubled from 11.8% to 24.3% between 1995 and 2015. However, the female share in paid employment fell sharply between 2000 and 2011, from 33.1% to 20.9%. While there has been an increase since 2011, recovery has been slow, with the female share in employment reaching just 26.5% in 2014.[12] In Mongolia, there has been a notable decline in female employment in the past 20 years.[13] This phenomenon has been attributed to Mongolia's rapid transition from a socialist to a market economy and the subsequent reliance on revenue from the male-dominated mining sector, coupled with the erosion of state-funded labor survey conducted by the Mongolian National Statistics Office, which cited that 21.3% of women cited childcare as the main reason for their economic inactivity, whereas only 1.4% of men cited this as a reason.[14]

35.   **Increased unpaid work by women.** The disproportionate female burden of unpaid care work—which includes cooking, cleaning, fetching water and fuel, and caring for young children and elderly relatives—and limited measures such as subsidized childcare and flexible working hours is a key factor affecting women's economic participation in many CAREC countries. For example, in Kazakhstan, women spend 17.1% of their time in unpaid care work, in addition to being economically active, while men devote only 7.1% to unpaid care work.[15]

---

[12]   Government of Pakistan, Bureau of Statistics. 2015. *Compendium on Gender Statistics of Pakistan, 2014.* Islamabad.

[13]   A. Schmillen and N. Sandig. 2018. *Perceptions of Precariousness. A Qualitative Study of Constraints Underlying Gender Disparities in Mongolia's Labor Market.* Washington, DC: World Bank.

[14]   Women were 15 times more likely than men to cite childcare as the main reason for their economic activity. Footnote 13.

[15]   Republic of Kazakhstan, Ministry of National Economy, Committee on Statistics. *Women and Men in Kazakhstan 2015.* Astana.

36.   **Low-paid women's work.** Data indicate that women in CAREC countries are concentrated in lower-paid sectors, including agriculture, education, health care, retail and wholesale, hospitality, catering, and other services, whereas men predominate in well-paid sectors such as finance, engineering, mining, energy, and transport. For example, in Kazakhstan, 71.4% of women are employed in the services sector compared with 52% of men.[16] In the Kyrgyz Republic, 83.6% of the low-paid health and social services workforce is female, while men account for 84.4% of employees in the higher-paid mining industry.[17] In Uzbekistan, the highest-paid sectors in 2016 were insurance and finance, both male-dominated sectors.[18] This is contributing to a significant gender wage gap in many CAREC countries. For example, in the Kyrgyz Republic, women received on average 75.3% of male wages in 2016,[19] and in Georgia, women earned 64% of male earnings in 2017.[20] In Pakistan, men earn more than women of all ages in all sectors. The wage gap increases exponentially in male-dominated sectors. During 2010–2011, men earned around 50% more than women in agriculture, forestry, hunting, and fishing, where women comprise one-third of the workforce, and this rose to 130% more than women in transport, storage, and communications where only 1% of the workforce is female (footnote 14).

37.   **Overrepresentation of women in the informal sector.** This is characterized by the International Labour Organization as "lack of secure employment and poor social protection; prevalence of hard forms of labour; low salary levels; absence of pensions and lack of opportunities for development and investment in human capital."[21] The nature of this work means that reliable statistics are not available for all countries but there is some available recent data. For example, in Mongolia at the end of 2013, an estimated 212,300 people were working in the informal sector, of whom 125,700 (59.2%) were male and 86,600 (40.8%) were female.[22] Among CAREC countries, Afghanistan, Azerbaijan, and Pakistan have the highest proportion of women contributing as unpaid family workers.[23]

38.   **Gender biases in hiring and promotion.** Women entering the paid labor market in CAREC countries are also more likely than men to encounter poor workplace equality standards. Available research and evidence gathered for ADB country gender assessments point to gender biases in hiring practices and promotion opportunities, and failures to implement national policies on paid maternity and paternity leave, flexible working arrangements, and equal pay. For example, in Georgia, prospective employers often favor male applicants or ask young women if they plan to get married or have children. In addition, many private sector companies only provide minimal maternity leave provision for women, despite their entitlement to 6 months' paid leave under the Georgian Gender Equality Law and Labor Code.[24] High rates of sexual harassment and abuse in workplaces have also been reported by female employees in CAREC countries. For example, a study conducted by the Mongolian Gender Equality Center in 2004 revealed that one in five women

---

[16]   Footnote 15.

[17]   ADB. 2019. *Kyrgyz Republic: Country Gender Assessment*. Manila.

[18]   ADB. 2018. *Uzbekistan Country Gender Assessment*. Manila.

[19]   Footnote 17.

[20]   ADB. 2018. *Georgia: Country Gender Assessment*. Manila.

[21]   International Labour Organization. 2009. *Work and Family: The Republic of Tajikistan*. Moscow. http://www.ilo.org/moscow/information-resources/publications/WCMS_312658/lang--en/index.htm.

[22]   Green Climate Fund. 2017. Gender Assessment. FP046: Renewable Energy Program. Mongolia; Japan International Cooperation Agency. 2013. *Gender Country Profile: Mongolia*. Ulaanbaatar.

[23]   ADB. 2017. *Promoting Inclusive Growth through Private Sector Development in Central and West Asia. Good Jobs for Inclusive Growth in Central and West Asia*. Manila.

[24]   Footnote 20.

had experienced sexual harassment and that one in three knew someone who had been harassed. A follow-up study in 2017 showed that little has changed in the past 13 years and indicated that harassment is often perpetrated by men in positions of power or authority in the workplace.[25]

2.   Women's Access to Economic Opportunities

39.   **Entrepreneurship.** The potential economic empowerment benefits of entrepreneurship for women have been well documented. Micro, small, and medium-sized enterprises (MSMEs) offer opportunities for women to work in flexible ways that fit with their other responsibilities, potentially provide significant income generation, and enhance women's business and leadership skills, resulting in empowerment and greater autonomy.[26] Stories of success from female entrepreneurs in Georgia who accessed small business loans and underwent training as part of an ADB-funded program provide useful insights into the positive impacts for women, their families, and their communities. For example, a Muslim woman living in a remote region of Georgia borrowed $5,660 to establish the first guesthouse in the region, which was a success.[27]

40.   Yet women continue to face both social and financial challenges in setting up and running a business. These include the following:[28]

    (i)   Limited access to finance, for reasons that include lack of collateral, banks' unwillingness to administer small loans, and unusually high interest rates. For example, in Pakistan, only 13% of women reported owning any assets, compared with 69% of men.[29]

    (ii)   Limited business capacity and access to relevant information and technology.

    (iii)   Gender norms and assumptions and sociocultural rules that undermine support and/or create barriers for women entrepreneurs—for example, in some countries, women require a husband's signature to obtain a loan. In Pakistan, sociocultural rules mean that more than 70% of women are not permitted to leave the house to visit a bank, and for those that are able to do so, 50% are not permitted to do so alone.[30]

    (iv)   The competing demands of unpaid care work.

    (v)   Lack of networking and organizing among female entrepreneurs, making it difficult for their voices and needs to be heard.

41.   Globally, around 80% of women-owned businesses with credit needs have little or no access to financial services, translating into a massive $1.7 trillion financing gap.[31]

---

[25]   T. Begzsuren and D. Aldar. 2014. *Gender Overview - Mongolia. Attitudes toward Gender Equality: A Survey Experiment in Mongolia.* Conducted by the Independent Research Institute of Mongolia (IRIM), as commissioned by the Swiss Agency for Development and Cooperation (SDC). https://www.eda.admin.ch/dam/countries/countries-content/mongolia/en/SDC-Gender-%20Overview-Mongolia-%202014-EN.pdf.

[26]   ADB. 2014. *Gender Tool Kit: Micro, Small, and Medium-Sized Enterprise Finance and Development.* Manila.

[27]   Footnote 20.

[28]   Footnote 26.

[29]   ADB. 2016. *Pakistan: Country Gender Assessment, vol. 1.* Manila.

[30]   Footnote 29.

[31]   International Finance Corporation. 2019. Banking on Women. https://www.ifc.org/wps/wcm/connect/Industry_EXT_Content/ IFC_External_Corporate_Site/Financial+Institutions/Priorities/Banking_on_Women/.

42.   Data collected in 2017 by the ADB on the Kyrgyz Republic indicate that women comprised less than half of all borrowers in partner banks, and that loans for female borrowers accounted for only 25%–43% of their total loan portfolio.[32]

43.   In Mongolia, in 2013, only 27% of women with primary and secondary education were taking advantage of self-employment compared with 40% of men, particularly in urban areas.[33]

44.   In Kazakhstan, women face more difficulties in accessing credit than men because of prejudice regarding their ability to repay loans, as well as difficulties drawing up business plans and providing collateral. This is due to women's limited financial knowledge and to the common practice of registering properties under the name of the husband or male head of household.[34]

45.   In Pakistan, microfinance institutions prefer lending to women, as they are thought to be more likely to use loan proceeds in ways that improve family welfare, and to repay loans.[35]

46.   In general, women are less likely than men to have bank accounts in CAREC countries. Although efforts have scaled by development agencies and countries' governments to get more women signed up for accounts, the gender gap remains. While there is no significant difference between men's and women's account ownership in some CAREC countries such as Azerbaijan, Mongolia or Uzbekistan; the gender gap is wide for others, such as Pakistan and Afghanistan. On the contrary, Georgia, Kazakhstan, and Mongolia percentage of adult women holding a bank account is higher than percentage of adult men. Figure 1 shows information on percentage of adult men and women holding a bank account in a financial institution in the CAREC countries in 2017.[36]

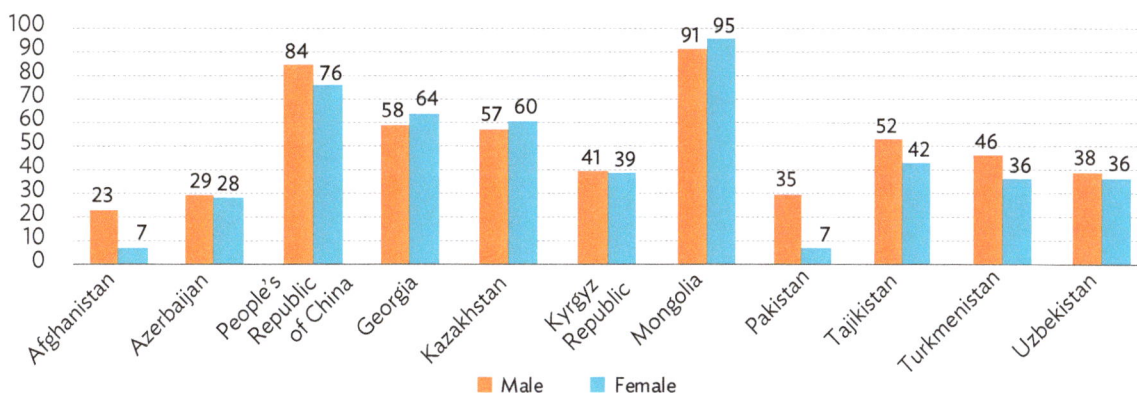

Figure 1: **Percentage of Adults of Each Gender Holding an Account with a Financial Institution in 2017**

Source: World Bank. 2017. *The Global Findex Database 2017: Measuring Financial Inclusion and the Fintech Revolution*. Washington, DC: World Bank Group. http://documents1.worldbank.org/curated/en/332881525873182837/pdf/126033-PUB-PUBLIC-pubdate-4-19-2018.pdf.

---

[32]   ADB. 2017. *Project Report: Consolidated Report on Gender Expertise of PFIs under ADB Women's Entrepreneurship Development Project*. Manila.

[33]   World Bank. 2013. *Mongolia: Gender Disparities in Labor Markets and Policy Suggestions*. Washington, DC.

[34]   ADB. 2018. *Kazakhstan Country Gender Assessment*. Manila.

[35]   From 2004 to 2012, women in Pakistan comprised over 45% of microfinance borrowers and, after a brief decline from 2006 to 2008, they increased to 63% of all borrowers by 2012. World Bank. 2013. *The Little Data Book on Gender 2013*. Washington, DC.

[36]   World Bank. The Global Findex Database 2017. https://globalfindex.worldbank.org/ (accessed 5 February 2021).

46.   In the first half of 2017, MSMEs in Uzbekistan accounted for 46% of the country's GDP, of which 42% are run by women. The Government of Uzbekistan provides support for women's entrepreneurship. However, the Uzbek case highlights the risk of restricting women to MSMEs and potentially missing opportunities to incorporate them into the formal labor market, where jobs are often more secure, better paid, and come with benefits such as paid sick and maternity leave, or failing to support them to scale up their businesses.[37] In Kazakhstan, MSMEs also play a crucial role in the economy, reaching 1.1 million in 2015. Of Kazakhstan's small and medium-sized enterprises, 42% was recorded in 2016 to be headed by women.[38]

47.   **Border trade.** Women in trade face several challenges, starting with time poverty. Time considerations, along with safety issues, prevent women from traveling long distances to explore new and more competitive markets. Women tend to travel by foot, making them more vulnerable to crime and physical danger. They are also less informed about market rules, which makes them more likely to become the targets of harassment or extortion by market and trade officials, impacting their motivation and well-being, and cutting into their time and profits.[39]

48.   According to some estimates, removing supply chain barriers in Central Asia and the South Caucasus would raise exports by 65%, imports by 49%, and the region's GDP by 8%.[40] Inclusion of women in supply chains can propel further growth.[41] Informal cross-border trading activities account for a significant portion of regional trade in countries along the CAREC corridors.[42] An example of this type of activity is "suitcase trading," a frequently used form of exchange in which traders cross the borders with their goods in a suitcase to evade border control, customs, and taxes.[43]

49.   Cross-border trade creates employment opportunities in border markets as well as in small informal businesses such as storage facilities, catering, hotels, and lodging. Often, attempts to formalize such operations have a negative impact on the livelihoods of small cross-border traders and entrepreneurs, who are typically women, unless their specific needs are catered to as part of the intervention. However, there are also many advantages, which include increased employment security, improved access to business services and networks, and increased access to relevant information and finances.

50.   **Tourism.** Women account for 54% of those employed in the tourism industry globally, and the figure is likely to be higher in some parts of Asia.[44] Tourism offers many potential opportunities for women, that include decent work,

[37]   ADB. 2018. *Uzbekistan Country Gender Assessment*. Manila.

[38]   DAMU Entrepreneurship Development Fund. 2016. *Report on the State of Development of Small and Medium Enterprises in Kazakhstan and its Regions*. Almaty.

[39]   K. Higgins. 2012. *Gender Dimensions of Trade Facilitation and Logistics: A Guidance Note*. Washington, DC. World Bank. https://openknowledge.worldbank.org/handle/10986/16973 License: CC BY 3.0 IGO.

[40]   World Economic Forum. 2014. *Scenarios for the South Caucasus and Central Asia*. http://www3.weforum.org/docs/WEF_Scenarios_SouthCaucasusCentralAsia_Report_2014.pdf.

[41]   N. Rillo and S. Nugroho. 2016. *Promoting Agricultural Value Chain Integration in Central Asia and the Caucasus*. ADB Institute. https://www.adb.org/sites/default/files/publication/214121/adbi-pb2016-4.pdf.

[42]   See, for example, H. Karrar. 2013. From Pastoral Nomadism to Shuttle Trade: A Long View of Modernity and Commerce along the Sino-Central Asian Border. In M. Gervers and G. Long, eds. *Material Culture, Language and Religion of Central and Inner Asia*. Toronto: Asian Institute, University of Toronto, Toronto Studies in Central and Inner Asia. pp. 207–219.

[43]   C. Humphrey. 2002. *The Unmaking of Soviet Economic Life: Everyday Economies after Socialism*. Ithaca: Cornell University Press; I. Mukhina. 2009. New Losses, New Opportunities: (Soviet) Women in Shuttle Trade, 1987–1998. *Journal of Social History*. 43 (2). pp. 341–359.

[44]   UN World Tourism Organization. 2019. Global Report on Women in Tourism - Second Edition. https://www.e-unwto.org/pb-assets/unwto/191121_action_plan_women_in_tourism_2nd_ed.pdf.

entrepreneurship, tourism education and training, and leadership and decision-making roles (footnote 33). In CAREC countries, women are engaged directly in the tourism industry and also provide other related services (for example, informal trading, handicraft production and sale, catering, guesthouses).[45] There is great potential to increase women's business and employment in the sector.[46] However, while tourism promotion and open visa regimes have many benefits, such measures can also have unintended consequences, such as increasing or encouraging human trafficking and sexual exploitation, with women often particularly at risk.[47] All CAREC countries have enacted legislation prohibiting human trafficking and protecting victims.[48] However, more concerted efforts are needed to tackle human trafficking in many CAREC countries.[49]

51.   **Agriculture.** An estimated 43% of women globally work in agriculture, a figure which is likely to be even higher in many CAREC countries.[50] According to the most recent figures gathered by the Food and Agriculture Organization of the United Nations (FAO), in 2010, 38.4% of the economically active population in Asia is female and 57.6% of these were engaged in agriculture. The numbers vary considerably according to specific regions. In Central Asia, of the 47% of women who were economically active, only 17.8% were engaged in agriculture, while in East Asia, 61.8% of the 45.5% of working women were farmers and in South Asia only 29.6% of women were economically active with 60.4% working in agriculture. In West Asia, only 35.8% of the 25.7% economically active women were farmers (see Table 4 for information on individual CAREC countries).[51]

52.   However, often this agriculture work is poorly paid or unpaid. Many women farmers face challenges that include limited access to productive resources such as land, water, seeds, and labor-saving tools, and to higher-value markets and information. The business case for investing in women working in agriculture has been set out, with the FAO stating: "Closing the gender gap in agriculture would generate significant gains for the agriculture sector and for society. If women had the same access to productive resources as men, they could increase yields on their farms by 20–30%. This could raise total agricultural output in developing countries by 2.5–4%."[52]

53.   Wage employment comprises only a small share of women's involvement in agriculture, and women are more likely to participate as contributing family workers (footnote 50). In some CAREC countries, women perform

---

[45]   See footnote 20; ADB. 2018. *Kazakhstan Country Gender Assessment.* Manila; ADB. 2018. *Uzbekistan Country Gender Assessment.* Manila; ADB. 2016. *Tajikistan: Country Gender Assessment.* Manila.

[46]   ADB. 2019. *Promoting Regional Tourism Cooperation under CAREC 2030: A Scoping Study.* www.carecprogram.org.

[47]   Uzbekistan has granted visa-free access to 101 countries starting from July 2018, and Pakistan launched an e-visa scheme for 175 countries in March 2019. The Silk Road visa, a joint initiative between Kazakhstan and Uzbekistan, is also underway. ADB. 2019. *Summary Poverty Reduction and Social Strategy, Hydropower Project, Uzbekistan.* Manila.

[48]   Article 113 of the Criminal Code (Mongolia); Law on Prevention and Combating Trafficking in Persons 2005 (Kyrgyz Republic); Article 129 of the Criminal Code 2010 (Turkmenistan); Prevention and Control of Human Trafficking Ordinance and Trafficking in Persons Act, 2018 (Pakistan); Articles 128, 133, 125(3)(b), 126(3)(b), and 270 of the Penal Code (Kazakhstan); Law on Countering Abduction and Human Trafficking 2008 (Afghanistan); On Countering Human Trafficking 2008 (Uzbekistan); Article 43 of the Criminal Code (Georgia); Law on the Fight Against Trafficking in Persons 2005, and Article 144 of the Criminal Code (Azerbaijan); Article 130.1 of the Criminal Code (Tajikistan); Signatory to UN protocols and various domestic laws (PRC).

[49]   For example, four CAREC countries are in Tier 2 of the Trafficking in Persons 2019 report watchlist for significant efforts but not meeting some of minimum standards (Azerbaijan, Kazakhstan, Kyrgyz Republic, Uzbekistan), while the PRC and Turkmenistan are in Tier 3, for not meeting minimum standards despite the enactment of laws. www.state.gov.

[50]   FAO. 2011. Women in Agriculture: Closing the Gender Gap for Development. *The State of Food and Agriculture, 2010–11.* http://www.fao.org/publications/sofa/2010-11/en/.

[51]   Footnote 50.

[52]   Footnote 50.

Table 4: Economically Active Population, Female Share of Economically Active Population, and Agricultural Share of Economically Active Women in 2010[a]

	Total of Economically Active Population ('000)	Female Share (% of total)	Agricultural Share of Economically Active Women (%)
World	**3,282,308**	**40.5**	**42.0**
Asia (excluding Japan)	**1,964,239**	**38.4**	**57.6**
Central Asia	**29,095**	**47.0**	**17.8**
Kazakhstan	8,427	49.8	6.8
Kyrgyz Republic	2,547	42.6	14.6
Tajikistan	2,896	46.8	31.1
Turkmenistan	2,437	47.1	33.4
Uzbekistan	12,788	46.2	20.2
East Asia (excluding Japan)	**855,786**	**45.5**	**61.8**
People's Republic of China	817,033	45.6	64.0
Mongolia	1,204	50.2	17.1
South Asia	**699,660**	**29.6**	**60.4**
Afghanistan	9,384	23.4	82.0
Pakistan	67,292	20.3	56.9
West Asia	**80,575**	**25.7**	**35.8**
Azerbaijan	4,633	47.9	25.6
Georgia	2,278	46.7	11.7

[a] These are the most recent comprehensive figures on women in agriculture for CAREC countries.

Source: Food and Agriculture Organization of the United Nations (FAO). 2011. Women in Agriculture: Closing the Gender Gap for Development. *The State of Food and Agriculture, 2010–11*. pp. 11–113.

manual labor in work such as food processing and packaging, and other value-added activities.[53] In CAREC countries, gender power asymmetries mean that women often lack control of assets and have restricted access to finance, as well as low participation in commercial and export-oriented markets and limited access to information.[54] This undermines the economic potential of women in agriculture. Promoting value chain integration and developing supply chains for agriculture are essential for growth in the sector, but the role of women has not been fully articulated.[55]

[53] ADB. Mongolia: Community Vegetable Farming for Livelihood Improvement. https://www.adb.org/projects/50278-001/main.

[54] ADB. 2019. *Strategy 2030 Operational Plan for Priority 2: Accelerating Progress in Gender Equality, 2019–2024*. Manila; ADB. Mongolia: Community Vegetable Farming for Livelihood Improvement. https://www.adb.org/projects/50278-001/main; ADB. Kyrgyz Republic: Climate Change and Disaster-Resilient Water Resources Sector Project. https://www.adb.org/projects/51081-002/main; ADB. 2018. *Georgia: Country Gender Assessment*.

[55] N. Rillo and S. Nugroho. 2016. Promoting Agricultural Value Chain Integration in Central Asia and the Caucasus. *ADBI Policy Brief*. No: 2016-4. Manila: ADB.

54.   Male labor migration in Central Asia over the last 2 decades has increased opportunities for women in agriculture beyond working as farm labor.[56] However, as women take on traditionally male agricultural occupations, the burden on them increases while they often remain excluded from the information and resource pools of local agriculture networks. For example, women farmers have increasing responsibility for water resource and irrigation management yet they often have limited representation in decision-making relating to water management.[57] For example, a 2013 study found that only 18% of water user association members in the Kyrgyz Republic were women.[58] In Pakistan, women often cannot participate in community decision-making about water as members of water user associations due to lack of land rights, illiteracy, agricultural and household workload, and social norms that block women from attending public meetings.[59]

3.   Women's Participation in Decision-Making

55.   In the majority of CAREC countries, women and men have equal rights under the law, but patriarchal gender roles and norms often have implications for household, community, and national-level decision-making. However, the picture for many countries is complex and nuanced, making it important to gain an in-depth understanding of women's decision-making power at all levels.

56.   In all CAREC countries, women have the right to participate in public life and hold public office, yet in all 11 countries, women's political participation falls well below the 33% advocated by the Beijing Platform for Action. The lowest female representation is in Georgia, at only 16% of seats, although this number has risen from only 6.4% in 2008.[60] Women in Uzbekistan and Azerbaijan have only 16.8% of seats and in Mongolia, 17.1%.[61] According to the 2019 GII figures, despite being the lowest ranked of CAREC countries, Afghanistan has the highest female representation of all the countries, at 27.4% of seats in Parliament. This can be largely attributed to Afghanistan's constitutional quota system, which reserves 68 out of 250 seats (27%) in Parliament for women. However, women wishing to go into government need financial resources and support from powerful allies such as warlords,[62] and once they are elected, they have little access to real decision-making power or spaces.[63] Representation in Parliament is also not reflected in other critical decision-making positions. Only 12% of judges and 7% of the staff of the High Court are female, with this figure declining from 15% in 2012.[64]

---

[56]   N. Mukhamedova. 2018. The Feminization of Agriculture in Post-Soviet Tajikistan. *Journal of Rural Studies*. Volume 57.

[57]   Farming First. 2018. *Why Women Are Key for Water Management in Tajikistan.* https://farmingfirst.org/2018/07/why-women-are-key-for-water-management-in-tajikistan; E. Kim. 2019. *Sustainability of Irrigation in Uzbekistan: Implications for Women Farmers. Water and Sustainability, February.* doi:10.5772/intechopen.79732; J. Memon et al. 2019. Mainstreaming Gender into Irrigation: Experiences from Pakistan. *Water.* 11 (11). doi:10.3390/w11112408; FAO. 2015. *The Role of Agricultural Innovation Systems in Central Asia and Caucasus Countries and China: Towards More Sustainable Food Security and Nutrition.* Proceedings of online discussion. http://www.fao.org/fsnforum/resources/outcomes/role-agricultural-innovation-systems-central-asia-and-caucasus-countries-and.

[58]   UNDP. 2013. *Climate Profile of the Kyrgyz Republic.* Bishkek. www.kg.undp.org.

[59]   ADB. 2016. *Pakistan Country Gender Assessment,* vol. 2. Manila.

[60]   Inter-Parliamentary Union. 2017. *Women in Politics.* https://www.ipu.org/resources/publications/infographics/2017-03/women-in-politics-2017.

[61]   UNDP. 2020. *Global Inequality Index.* http://hdr.undp.org/en/content/gender-inequality-index-gii.

[62]   Afghanistan Analysts Network. 2018. *Afghanistan Elections Conundrum (20): Women Candidates Going against the Grain.* https://www.afghanistan-analysts.org/en/reports/political-landscape/afghanistan-elections-conundrum-19-women-candidates-going-against-the-grai.

[63]   A. Larson. 2016. *Women and Power: Mobilising around Afghanistan's Elimination of Violence Against Women Law.* London: Overseas Development Institute.

[64]   Japan International Cooperation Agency. 2013. *Country Gender Profile: Afghanistan.* Tokyo.

57.   Pakistan has a history of creating political quotas for women, beginning in 1947 at 3% and rising to 17% in 2002 in both national and provincial assemblies.[65] Since then the proportion of seats held by women in the National Assembly and Senate has remained at around 20%.[66] However, these female politicians are not representative of the majority of Pakistani women, as the allocated seats often go to women from influential political families. The cases of Afghanistan and Pakistan illustrate that, while quotas can guarantee a critical mass of women in politics, considerable work is needed to ensure this translates into meaningful influencing power.

58.   Evidence indicates that women in CAREC countries are also encountering a "glass ceiling" with regard to decision-making in public sector institutions and private sector companies. Most of the 11 countries fare poorly in terms of the proportion of women in managerial positions. According to the United Nations Economic and Social Commission for Asia and the Pacific SDG Database, of CAREC countries included in 2017, Mongolia had the highest rate of women in managerial positions (40.8%), followed by the Kyrgyz Republic (36.2%) and Azerbaijan (34.5%), with Pakistan at only 2.9%.[67] One clear exception is the PRC, where an estimate of more than 50% of senior management positions in private companies are held by women, for reasons that may include state encouragement of women's employment and the rapid growth in female entrepreneurship. This puts the PRC far above the global average of 24%.[68] See Figure 2 for information on female participation in firms and businesses in CAREC countries.

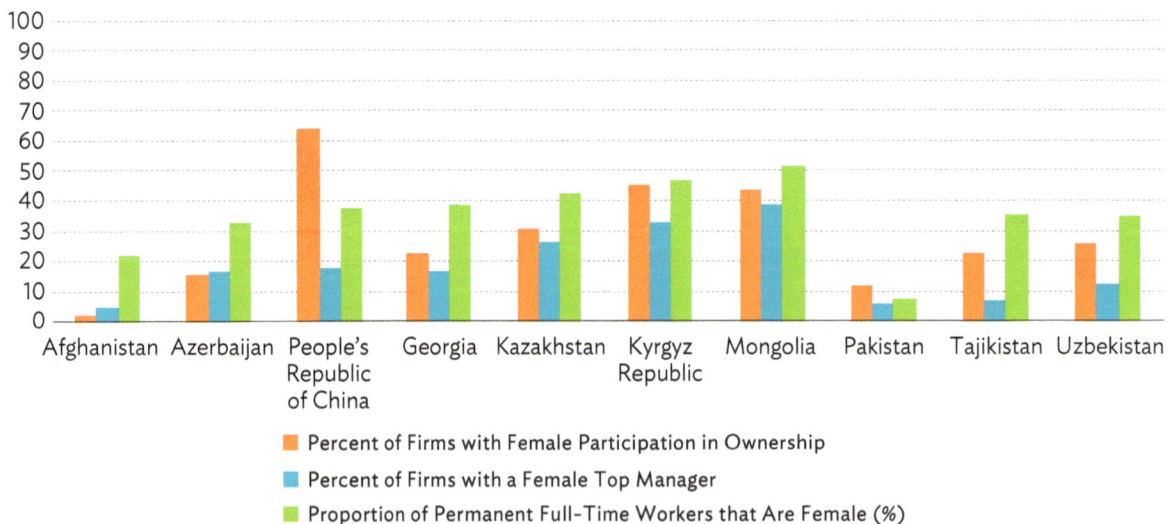

Figure 2: Gender Indicators Related to Female Participation in Firms and Businesses in CAREC Countries

- Percent of Firms with Female Participation in Ownership
- Percent of Firms with a Female Top Manager
- Proportion of Permanent Full-Time Workers that Are Female (%)

CAREC = Central Asia Regional Economic Cooperation.
Note: Data from 2019, except for Afghanistan (2014), PRC (2012), and Pakistan (2013). No available data for Turkmenistan in this database.
Source: World Bank. Enterprise Surveys. http://www.enterprisesurveys.org. (accessed 5 February 2021).

[65]   M. Awan. 2018. *Political Participation of Women in Pakistan Historical and Political Dynamics Shaping the Structure of Politics for Women.* Germany: Frankfurter Forschungszentrum Globaler Islam. www.researchgate.net.

[66]   Aurat Foundation. 2003. *Legislative Watch.* 18–19 (February); Aurat Foundation. 2008. *Legislative Watch.* 23 (January–March); Aurat Foundation. 2013. *Legislative Watch.* 41 (March–December).

[67]   United Nations. SDG Indicators. https://unstats.un.org/sdgs/indicators/database (accessed June 2020).

[68]   A. Mahajan. 2013. China: Setting the New Standard for Women in Top Jobs? *The Guardian.* 25 September. https://www.theguardian.com/women-in-leadership/2013/sep/25/china-uk-female-senior-managers-study.

4.   Women's and Girls' Access to Education and Training

59.   As the GII figures indicate, the majority of CAREC countries have achieved gender parity or near parity in primary and secondary education. However, the clear exceptions are Pakistan, where nearly 50% more boys than girls have received a secondary education, and Afghanistan, where girls account for around one-third of secondary school students. A 2012 report found that dropout rate among girls in Afghanistan was 31%, considerably higher than for boys at 13%.[69] This phenomenon can be largely attributed to the fact that many parents do not believe that sending their daughters to school beyond primary school is important.[70] By contrast, in Mongolia and Tajikistan, boys are less likely than girls to complete secondary school and enter tertiary education. For example, in the academic year 2013/14, almost two-thirds of all graduates were women. The "reverse gender gap" in Mongolia is largely due to parents removing boys from school temporarily or permanently so they can contribute to herding and other work to support the family income.[71]

60.   Despite the growing number of women with secondary and tertiary education in many CAREC countries, they still lag far behind in science, technology, engineering, and mathematics (STEM) subjects. In Tajikistan, for example, men comprised virtually 100% of the student population in technical subjects for the academic year 2013/14.[72] In Kazakhstan, men accounted for 100% of enrollment in electrical engineering and transport technology during the academic year 2011/12.[73] It appears that gender norms and perceptions strongly influence female students' choice of field in CAREC countries. For example, in Georgia, only around a quarter of women are studying engineering, manufacturing, and construction, but they comprise 80% of arts and humanities students and 70% of those studying health at the tertiary level.[74] In the Kyrgyz Republic, women and girls often choose traditionally female-dominated fields such as education, garment making, or food processing.[75]

5.   Women's and Girls' Access to Health Services

61.   There has been a steady improvement across health indicators for CAREC countries, but there is continued poor access to health services in some countries, particularly those ranked as having low or medium human development in the Human Development Index, which is reflected in a relatively high maternal mortality ratio (MMR). Afghanistan falls into the low development category and is ranked the lowest of all CAREC countries, at 170. It also has by far the highest MMR of all CAREC countries, with 638 maternal deaths out of 100,000 live births registered in 2017. This can be attributed to the fact that many areas still have no access to basic health care facilities or trained health professionals—particularly female doctors, obstetricians, and gynecologists—with rural areas being extremely badly served. As a result, a high number of women still give birth at home without a skilled birth attendant.[76]

---

[69] S. Hall. 2013. Increasing the Access and Quality of Basic Education for Marginalized Girls in Faryab. Afghanistan: ACTED.

[70] Footnote 64.

[71] Government of Mongolia/UNDP. 2013. *Achieving the Millennium Development Goals: Fifth National Review Report*. Ulaanbaatar.

[72] ADB. 2016. *Tajikistan Country Gender Assessment*. Manila.

[73] ADB. 2018. *Kazakhstan Country Gender Assessment*. Manila.

[74] Footnote 20.

[75] Footnote 17.

[76] Footnote 64.

At the other end of the scale is Turkmenistan, which has an MMR of 7, followed by Kazakhstan with 10 maternal deaths out of every 100,000 registered in 2017.[77]

62.   Evidence indicates that targeted investments can make a marked difference to health outcomes. For example, after investing considerably in improvements to maternal health,[78] Azerbaijan decreased its MMR from 47 in 2000 to 25 in 2020,[79] while average life expectancy has risen from 66.8 in 2000 to 72.9 in 2018.[80]

6.   Women's and Girls' Access to Information and Communication Technology

63.   According to some estimates, by 2022, approximately 60% of global GDP will be digitized.[81] Digital technology is a key entry point for improving women's access to finance and catalyzing economic participation. There are two main challenges in relation to digital inclusion in CAREC countries: (i) improving access to ICT and services for all, and (ii) reducing the gender gap in digital inclusion. With the exception of the PRC and Kazakhstan, the quality of digital services is poor in all countries and the cost of access is high.[82] Across all 11 CAREC countries, women have less access than men to ICT. A 2019 global study indicated that mobile phones are the main means of internet access in low- and middle-income countries, particularly for women. Yet, at the same time, men in low- and middle-income countries are 10% more likely than women to own a mobile phone, which means that 197 million fewer women than men own a mobile phone.[83] There is no specific data for CAREC countries, but the same study found that in Europe and Central Asia, 90% of women own mobile phones, while 17 million women remain unconnected. These figures are lower than for any other global region but do not take into account the specific socioeconomic situations of Central Asian CAREC countries. In East Asia and the Pacific, 93% of women own mobile phones while 54 million remain unconnected, although in the PRC there is near gender parity in mobile internet usage (at 82% of men and 81% of women). In South Asia, only 27% of women use mobile internet, compared with the global average of 48%, putting South Asia far behind all other regions of the world in terms of gender-equitable access to ICT. The gender gap for Pakistan is even wider, although there is overall low use of mobile internet, with only 11% of women and 38% of men being mobile internet users (footnote 59).

64.   This gender disparity in access to ICT has multiple implications for women. Groups such as female entrepreneurs may be particularly disadvantaged, given the role that ICT plays in accelerating business growth.[84]

---

[77]   UNICEF Data. 2019. Trends in Estimates of Maternal Mortality Ratio (MMR), Maternal Deaths and Lifetime Risk of Maternal Death, 2000–2017. https://data.unicef.org/resources/dataset/maternal-mortality-data/.

[78]   ADB. 2019. *Azerbaijan: Country Gender Assessment*. Manila.

[79]   World Health Organization. 2018. *Maternal Mortality in 2000–2017: Azerbaijan.* https://www.who.int/gho/maternal_health/countries/aze.pdf?ua=1.

[80]   UNDP. 2019. *Human Development Report 2019. Inequalities in Human Development in the 21st Century. Briefing Note for Countries on the 2019 Human Development Report: Azerbaijan.* http://hdr.undp.org/sites/all/themes/hdr_theme/country-notes/AZE.pdf.

[81]   World Economic Forum. 2018. *Our Shared Digital Future: Building an Inclusive, Trustworthy and Sustainable Digital Society.* https://www.weforum.org/reports/our-shared-digital-future-building-an-inclusive-trustworthy-and-sustainable-digital-society.

[82]   World Bank. 2017. *Central and South Asia: Disconnected in the Digital Age.* Presentation for Digital Central Asia South Asia (CASA) Programme. Sixth session of the Asia-Pacific Information Superhighway (AP-IS) Steering Committee, Dhaka. https://www.unescap.org/sites/default/files/Digital%20Central%20Asia%20South%20Asia%20%28CASA%29%20Program%2C%20World%20Bank.pdf.

[83]   GSMA. 2019. *Connected Women: The Mobile Gender Gap Report 2019.* https://www.gsma.com/mobilefordevelopment/wp-content/uploads/2019/03/GSMA-Connected-Women-The-Mobile-Gender-Gap-Report-2019.pdf.

[84]   ADB. 2014. *Information and Communication Technologies for Women Entrepreneurs: Prospects and Potential in Azerbaijan, Kazakhstan, the Kyrgyz Republic, and Uzbekistan.* Manila.

7.   Women's Access to Infrastructure and Public Services

65.   **Transport.** There is a widespread assumption that women and men benefit equally from transport projects and use travel infrastructure in similar ways. However, there are often significant gender differences in trip patterns and mobility constraints in CAREC countries, resulting in gender differences in the purpose of travel and mode of transport used.[85] For example, a 2007 time use survey by the Pakistan Bureau of Statistics and UNDP mapping daily diary records of 37,830 respondents aged 11 years and above found that women made fewer daily trips (2.8) than men (5.4), and that women's trips were, on average, 44% shorter than men's.[86] Women in CAREC countries are also less likely to drive and own a vehicle than men. For example, in Georgia, fewer than half of registered drivers in 2016 were female.[87] For many women in developing countries, walking is the main mean of transport. The use of others, such as public transport, are limited due to high prices, access difficulties, and unsafety.[88] Women farmers in rural communities may be more reliant on small feeder roads for transporting goods to market.

66.   Women are also more likely to use public transport than men for reasons that include commuting to work, and undertaking tasks related to their roles as primary caregivers such as food shopping, taking children to school, and going to clinics. Yet these services are often insufficient and fail to respond to the specific needs of women and vulnerable groups such as the elderly. Lack of access to public transport hinders access to work, particularly for women, and affects school attendance for students.[89] For example, in Uzbekistan, there is insufficient public transport in many rural areas. Private minibuses and taxis are the most common modes of transport, but they are costly and often not safe.

67.   In Afghanistan and Pakistan, religious and cultural gender norms often affect women's mobility. In both countries, many women are not permitted to travel outside their village or home or are required to have an escort to do so.[90] They are prohibited from sitting next to men other than their family members, which restricts their capacity to use public transport that is not designed with their specific needs in mind.[91] In cases where female entrepreneurs in Afghanistan were able to enjoy greater mobility, this as required the resources to afford private cars and drivers. These factors considerably undermine women's capacity to participate in economic activities.[92]

68.   It is particularly important to integrate measures that address and reduce the risk of sexual and other forms of harassment for women using public transport, given the extent to which this has been reported as a growing problem in many CAREC countries.[93] For example, an ADB study of 230 women who used public transport in Karachi, Pakistan found that 85% of working women and 82% of students interviewed had been subjected to harassment by male passengers

---

[85]   ADB. 2013. *Gender and Transport Tool Kit: Maximizing the Benefits of Mobility for All.* Manila.

[86]   Adeel et al. 2013. *Gender, Mobility and Travel Behavior in Pakistan: Analysis of 2007 Time Use Survey.* Munich Personal RePEc Achive. Germany.

[87]   In 2016, 31,503 licenses were issued to women, compared to 63,919 issued to men. Only 154,481 cars are registered to women, compared to 872,014 registered to men. National Statistics Office. 2017. Footnote 20.

[88]   Footnote 85.

[89]   Food and Agriculture Organization of the United Nations or FAO. 2017. *Gender, Rural Livelihoods and Forestry. Socio-economic and Gender Analysis of Forestry Sector in Uzbekistan.* Tashkent, Uzbekistan.

[90]   Footnote 64.; Footnote 29.

[91]   ADB. 2015. A Safe Public Transportation System for Women and Girls. *Policy Brief.* Manila.

[92]   Footnote 64.; Footnote 29.

[93]   Footnote 91.

and sometimes by bus drivers or bus conductors on public transport.[94] A 2015 ADB study in Azerbaijan, Georgia, and Pakistan found that an overall average of 69% of respondents had experienced sexual harassment while using public transport in the past 6 months. The majority of these women did not receive help when they needed it, and many reduced their use of public transport as a result of the harassment.[95]

69.   In addition, the transport sector itself is a potential source of employment for women but in practice in many CAREC countries women are less likely to apply for the better-paid technical positions because they often lack training in STEM subjects. For example, in the Kyrgyz Republic, only 4.9% of all those employed in the transport and cargo sector in 2019 were women, only around 10% of trolleybus drivers were female.[96]

70.   **Energy.** Access to affordable, reliable, sustainable, and modern energy is essential for human development. "Energy poverty," which is one aspect of broader economic poverty, affects some CAREC countries.[97] In Pakistan, for example, three-quarters of all households were connected to the electricity grid by 2011 and household use was estimated to account for about 50% of total electricity consumption.[98] However, biofuels remain the main or supplementary source of energy for around 90% of rural and 50% of urban households, and women often have primary responsibility for collecting them.[99] Tajikistan relies almost completely on domestic hydropower, but water supplies are often lowest in winter, when demand for electricity is highest. As a result, most households receive electricity for only 3–7 hours per day during the winter, so they often need to supplement their energy with solid and fossil fuels.

71.   Energy poverty has an impact on women and girls due to the toll it takes on their time, especially as it often falls to them to collect fuel or prepare stoves for cooking and heating, resulting in "time poverty."[100] In more remote areas, deforestation means that women and children are obliged to travel 15 kilometers or more to collect fuel. In some cases, girls are forced to drop out from school to assist in household tasks, including collection of biofuels.[101] Fuel collection also carries risks of sexual harassment or abuse for women and girls who have to travel long distances from home.[102]

72.   Women's and children's health is also more likely to be negatively affected by poor air quality in homes due to burning biofuels.[103] An improved and more efficient energy supply can, therefore, lead to both improved health outcomes and economic empowerment, freeing up time for women to seek employment or engage in other economic activities.[104]

---

[94]   ADB. 2014. *Rapid Assessment of Sexual Harassment in Public Transportation and Connected Spaces in Karachi.* Manila. https://www.adb.org/sites/default/files/project-document/152881/44067-012-tacr-19.pdf.

[95]   Footnote 91.

[96]   Footnote 17.

[97]   These countries include members of the former Soviet Union and outer Mongolia.

[98]   C. Trimble, N. Yoshida, and M. Saqib. 2011. *Rethinking Electricity Tariffs and Subsidies in Pakistan.* Washington, DC: World Bank.

[99]   Footnote 29.

[100]   UN Women and World Bank. 2018. *Policy Brief 12: Global Progress of SDG 7—Energy and Gender.* https://sustainabledevelopment.un.org/content/documents/17489PB12.pdf.

[101]   ADB. 2016. *Tajikistan: Country Gender Assessment.* Manila.

[102]   Footnote 29.

[103]   ADB. 2012. *Gender Tool Kit. Energy: Going Beyond the Meter.* Manila.

[104]   T. Khitarishvili. 2016. *Gender Inequalities in Labour Markets in Central Asia.* New York: UNDP.

73.   The energy sector could also provide a useful source of employment for women, particularly in the growing sustainable energy market. There are increasing good examples of female capacity building and small businesses in renewable energy such as solar power. For example, the Agency for Technical Cooperation and Development (ACTED), Pakistan, implemented an initiative that provided technical training in solar energy to promote sustainable solutions for women's empowerment. With support from ADB, ACTED trained 54 women in Multan, Punjab, in Pakistan as solar technicians.[105] Additionally, a clear indirect impact of providing a reliable, affordable, and accessible energy supply for households is that it improves the capacity of women to run small businesses such as tailoring or food preparation.[106]

74.   However, available data indicate that in many CAREC countries, technical occupations in sectors such as energy are dominated by men.[107] For example, the energy sector plays a critical role in Azerbaijan's socioeconomic growth, accounting for around 50% of the country's GDP, but only 11.3% of those employed in electricity, gas, and steam production are women. Women comprise only 13% of students taking up energy-related subjects.

75.   **Water.** Challenges in providing universal access to reliable household-level services, such as water and energy, vary across CAREC countries and within countries, between urban centers and rural areas. In CAREC countries, women often have the primary responsibility for water management for the household and are thus disproportionately burdened by water supply and quality issues. In many CAREC countries, old and inadequate water supply infrastructure is being replaced or renovated with funding from ADB and other funders, but reliance on the existing systems continues in the meantime. For example, Uzbekistan inherited excellent water supply and sanitation infrastructure, but the system is not only outdated, it has also been damaged by corrosion and inefficient use. This results in a lack of continuity in water services, insufficient water pressure, and chronic shortages of potable water.[108] Uzbek women are the main collectors, users, and managers of water for households. In rural areas, women (and often children) are required to collect drinking water several times a day from canals, springs, or sometimes a pump, for a total of 22 person-hours per month. Women also spend time boiling water so that it is safe to drink.[109]

76.   Evidence from ADB projects illustrates the direct and indirect benefits to women and their families of access to a modern, reliable water supply in the home. For example, women in the town of Poti, Georgia, reported that before the installation of a clean water plant delivering running water directly to their homes, the limited and poor water supply meant they were obliged to wake up at 2 or 3 a.m. in order to collect and store water for the week. The poor quality of water also meant they needed to wash clothes by hand.[110] In many border areas, shared water resources are divided by international borders, creating additional difficulties for women. In Azerbaijan, women interviewed during a project mission conducted for the ADB Water Supply and Sanitation Investment Program in October 2017 also noted that having access to a 24-hour supply significantly reduced their time poverty, as they no longer needed to collect water from outside sources and could drink the water rather than spending time boiling, filtering, or sterilizing it. They are now also able to use washing machines rather than washing by hand, which was necessary previously because of the high level of mineral deposits in the water.[111]

---

[105]   ADB. 2018. *Solar Energy Training Brightens Up Employment Opportunities for Pakistan's Women*. Manila.
        https://www.adb.org/news/videos/solar-energy-training-brightens-employment-opportunities-pakistan-s-women.

[106]   ACTED. 2012. *Transcend Traditions: Pakistani Women at the Forefront of Solar Energy Promotion*. Pakistan.
        https://www.acted.org/en/transcend-traditions-pakistani-women-at-the-forefront-of-solar-energy-promotion/.

[107]   See ADB's country gender assessments for Georgia, Kazakhstan, Uzbekistan, and Tajikistan.

[108]   ADB. 2017. *Poverty and Social Analysis: Western Uzbekistan Water Supply System Development Project*. Manila.

[109]   ADB. 2018. *Uzbekistan Country Gender Assessment: Update*. Manila.

[110]   Footnote 20.

[111]   Footnote 78.

## CHAPTER III

GENDER INCLUSION ANALYSIS OF CAREC PROJECTS

77.   This chapter includes the findings of a comprehensive analysis of selected 107 CAREC projects implemented between 2014 and 2018, to identify gaps and missed opportunities in gender mainstreaming. This sample includes country-specific and regional projects implemented in all 11 CAREC countries, through loans and technical assistance, and by different CAREC development partners, such as ADB, the European Bank for Reconstruction and Development (EBRD), Global Environment Facility (GEF), the Islamic Development Bank, the UNDP, and the World Bank. The full list of projects reviewed can be found in Appendix 1.

78.   The analysis focused on the following:

(i)   Gender-responsive practices and features of CAREC transport, energy, and trade projects, which were selected for the research sample as these have been the main sectors for CAREC operations since the program's inception in 2001—as well as missed opportunities.[112]

(ii)   Potential gender design features for specific CAREC subsectors and recommendations for future planning and implementation.

79.   Since the majority of these initiatives (91 out of 108) are ADB projects, the assessment refers to ADB's system of categories in which projects are classified according to the degree to which gender elements are included (Box 1).

Box 1: ADB Gender Categories

■   **GEN** – Gender equity. It is applied to a project if its outcome directly addresses gender disparities.

■   **EGM** – Effective gender mainstreaming. It is applied to a project if the majority of its outputs directly improve women's access to social services, economic resources, and infrastructure benefits, or enhance women's rights and decision-making.

■   **SGE** – Some gender elements. It is applied to a project if less than half of its outputs have some direct gender benefits.

■   **NGE** – No gender elements. It is applied to a project if it has only indirect gender benefits.

Source: ADB. 2012. *Guidelines for Gender Mainstreaming Categories of ADB Projects*. Manila.

---

[112]   The CAREC 2030 strategy selectively extended operations to five operational clusters, however, since many of the projects under these have not yet been implemented, the research for this assessment focused on the three sectors in order to analyze how the program has responded to gender issues.

80.   A classification of the reviewed CAREC projects according to ADB gender categories can be found in Table 5. Although some promising good practices are emerging, there is considerable scope to improve, scale up, and mainstream gender inclusion and gender sensitivity in programs and projects across CAREC countries.

Table 5: Summary of CAREC Projects Reviewed

Sector	Total	Gender Equity	Effective Gender Mainstreaming (ADB)	Some Gender Elements (ADB)	No Gender Elements (ADB)	Other Funding Sources
Transport	64	0	9	20	28	7
Energy	26	0	1	5	10	10
Trade	11	0	0	1	10	0
Multisector	6	0	0	0	6	0
Total	107	0	10	26	54	17

ADB = Asian Development Bank, CAREC = Central Asia Regional Economic Cooperation.

Source: Consultant under Asian Development Bank. 2020.

A. Gender Analysis of CAREC Transport Projects

81.   As noted above, the largest number of projects in the CAREC portfolio are in the transport sector. Of the 64 ADB-funded projects in the 2014–2018 transport portfolio, 29 are classified as effective gender mainstreaming (EGM) or some gender elements (SGE) and none are classified as gender equity (GEN). Seven projects funded by other organizations (EBRD, Islamic Development Bank, and World Bank) also contain gender elements. In some cases, projects classified as SGE, the gender-responsive features are nonexistent or minimal.

82.   However, there are multiple examples of good or emerging good practice, which are summarized in the sections below. As the transport projects are so numerous, good practice examples under the transport sector have been collated and organized in Appendix 2 as a reference tool.

83.   The remaining 28 transport projects, all ADB-funded, are categorized as no gender elements (NGE).[113] Many of the project documents for these initiatives refer to cultural barriers that prevent women from participating in consultations, for example in Afghanistan, or from being employed in CAREC projects (again in Afghanistan and also Pakistan).

84.   The majority of the projects within the CAREC transport portfolio focus on **highway development**. One EBRD-funded project is related to **aviation**, and eight projects involve investment in the **railway** subsector. Of the eight rail projects in the transport portfolio for 2014–2018, the proposed project in Turkmenistan is the only railway project that is categorized as EGM. Generally, a multimodal transport system with public transport integration provides more opportunities and more flexibility for building in gender concerns.[114]

---

[113] Eight NGE projects are in Pakistan, five of which are road transport-related; three are in Uzbekistan (road transport); four are in Azerbaijan (three road, one rail-related); four are in Afghanistan (three road, one transport policies); five are regional (three road-related and two transport policies); two are in the Kyrgyz Republic (road-related), while Mongolia and Georgia each have one NGE project.

[114] Sustainable Mobility for All. 2017. *Global Mobility Report 2017*. https://openknowledge.worldbank.org/bitstream/handle/10986/28542/120500.pdf?sequence=6.

85.   All **regional projects** for 2014–2018 were categorized as NGE. Many of them have conducted scoping studies and developed subsector strategies to be jointly implemented across CAREC countries. Gender concerns were not considered in the strategy documents. Some scoping studies contained gender elements, such as the Aviation and Role of CAREC Scoping Study,[115] which recognizes aviation as key enabler for skilled employment, and the Decision Makers Guide to Road Tolling in CAREC Countries ,[116] which notes that job opportunities for women are to be created, but on the whole, the omission of gender issues from regional projects was a missed opportunity.

1.   Gender-Responsive Design Features of ADB-Funded CAREC Transport Projects

86.   The **economic empowerment** of women is an essential component of the CAREC 2030 vision. Elements related to economic empowerment are included in just eight transport projects. However, eight EGM and SGE projects—seven ADB and one World Bank—include strong economic empowerment pathways, which can be replicated in other projects (Appendix 2). These include identifying targets for women's involvement in public works, technical positions, and other transport-related roles, building women's capacity in technical areas, and promoting gender-equitable hiring practices. Promoting entrepreneurship among women and providing access to finance is also included in many ADB-supported transport projects. For example, the North–South Corridor (Kvesheti–Kobi) Road Project (2018) in Georgia aims to create opportunities for women's entrepreneurship. Within the CAREC transport portfolio, most economic empowerment activities focus on women's entrepreneurship programs (two projects) and access to finance for women (two projects), along with income-earning opportunities during construction (seven projects). Given the context of burgeoning women-led and women-based small and medium-sized enterprises, more projects in the future could incorporate entrepreneurship and financial inclusion aspects.

87.   Several projects serve as good examples of **amplifying women's voices** through involvement of women in consultations and other inclusive planning and needs-testing strategies (Appendix 2). However, more opportunities could be identified to improve the quality of gender inclusion. For example, in the Qaiser–Bari Dum Road Project in Afghanistan, classified as SGE, the gender and social dimension was considered in the implementation of small, community-level initiatives such as access roads, community centers, clinics, and schools, which is not the primary focus of the project.[117]

88.   Eight transport projects (in Afghanistan, Azerbaijan, Georgia, Kazakhstan, the Kyrgyz Republic, Mongolia, Tajikistan, and Uzbekistan) include gender-sensitive safety and resilience measures. These include road safety awareness-raising aimed at both women and men; installation of safety features such as crosswalks, safety signs, paved sidewalks, lighting, and separate toilets for women and men; and measures to prevent negative impacts along roads such as trafficking and sexual harassment (Appendix 2).

89.   The majority of ADB-funded CAREC transport projects have **due diligence strategies** in place, which identify opportunities and gaps for gender-responsive planning. Georgia, Kazakhstan, the Kyrgyz Republic, Tajikistan, and Uzbekistan have **systems in place for collecting and analyzing gender-disaggregated data** to inform design and monitor

---

[115]   ADB. 2018. *Aviation and the Role of CAREC: A Scoping Study*. Manila.

[116]   ADB. 2018. *Decision Makers Guide to Road Tolling in CAREC Countries*. Manila.

[117]   ADB. 2017. *Qaisar-Dari Bum Road Project, Afghanistan. Summary Poverty Reduction and Social Strategy*. Manila.

and evaluate indicators that include the effects of land acquisition, the economic empowerment of women, and the parties involved in road accidents. The majority of countries are developing **gender action plans** linked to specific projects. Four countries (Georgia, the Kyrgyz Republic, Tajikistan, and Uzbekistan) are supporting the **training of project and ministry staff** in technical areas relating to transport. The Peshawar Sustainable Bus Rapid Transit Corridor Project in Pakistan is another example of good practice on a transport project by ADB (Box 2).

Box 2: Good Practice on a Transport Project by ADB

The Peshawar Sustainable Bus Rapid Transit Corridor Project, in Pakistan, responded to gender issues that limit women's use of public transport. A gender analysis of men's and women's travel patterns showed that only 15% of women were using existing public transport due to the high risk of harassment from fellow passengers and discrimination from conductors and drivers. Another study found that 90% of women felt unsafe using existing bus services, and 25% of skilled and educated women were unable to work due to unsafe transport services. They also found the current buses uncomfortable and inadequate for their needs, particularly for elderly passengers and those traveling with children. As a result, many women have been choosing to walk up to 2 kilometers or pay for expensive private forms of transport rather than taking public transport.

The new transit stations include gender-sensitive features such as separate restrooms for women and men, separate ticketing counters and vending machines for women and men, and priority e-ticketing counters for the elderly and persons with disabilities. All buses have separate zones for women, children, elderly people, and persons with disabilities that are enforced by the bus staff. A Safe Travel Program will address the issues of sexual harassment, theft, bullying, and other security issues, including all forms of harassment against women, the elderly, children, persons with disabilities, and other vulnerable groups. Mechanisms will be put in place to address all complaints, whether directly experienced or observed by others.

Source: ADB. 2019. *Pakistan: Peshawar Sustainable Bus Rapid Transit Corridor Project*. Manila. https://www.adb.org/projects/48289-002/main#project-documents.

---

2.   Gender-Responsive Design Features of Other Funders' CAREC Transport Projects

90.   Among transport projects, the World Bank–funded Third Phase of the Central Asia Regional Links Programme[118] takes an integrated approach and is a gender-tagged project in the World Bank system. Thus, the result framework has indicators to monitor proposed actions to mitigate gender gaps identified by the project. The project's proposed development objective is to increase regional connectivity and support sustainable tourism development in the Kyrgyz Republic. It involves women in community-based tourism and other tourism-related activities, in the trade of agricultural products, and in training for civil aviation at the Kyrgyz Aviation Institute. The project also coordinates with another CAREC development partner, the Islamic Development Bank. As such, this is a good project to track for its integrated approach (road transport, aviation, tourism, and trade) while involving women as direct stakeholders. Another good practice by the World Bank is presented in Box 3.

---

[118] World Bank. 2018. *Third Phase of the Central Asia Regional Links Program*. Washington, DC.

> **Box 3: Good Practice on a Transport Project by the World Bank**
>
> The project paper of the World Bank Third Highway Project in Azerbaijan includes a social inclusion and gender component. During stakeholders' consultations, the views and opinions of different categories of road users were collected, analyzed, and incorporated into the road design. Particular attention was paid to ensuring accessibility and response to groups at risk of marginalization—for example, women and people with disabilities. The consultations found that women tended to have more complex trip patterns and perceptions of mobility and accessibility than men. These aspects had not been considered in earlier road transport projects in Azerbaijan. The design integrated these findings by paying particular attention to ensuring accessibility and response to groups at risk of marginalization—for example, women and the disabled. Examples of how social inclusion will be realized include the following:
>
> (i)   Development of a communication strategy aimed at disseminating information to groups at risk of marginalization.
>
> (ii)   Gender disaggregation of data from the road users' satisfaction survey in an effort to identify any differences between men and women in road usage and safety.
>
> Source: World Bank. 2016. *Project Paper on a Proposed Additional Loan in the Amount of US$ 140 Million to the Republic of Azerbaijan and Restructuring for a Third Highway Project.* documents.worldbank.org/curated/en/808581468197388982/pdf/PAD1626-P118023-P156377-R2016-0051-1-Box394870B-OUO-9.pdf.

B. Gender Analysis of CAREC Energy Projects

1.   Gender-Responsive Design Features of ADB-Funded CAREC Energy Projects

91.   A total of 26 CAREC energy projects were reviewed. Of the 16 ADB-funded projects, 10 (four in Afghanistan, one in Tajikistan, one in Turkmenistan, two in the Kyrgyz Republic, and two regional projects) are classified as NGE. Six projects are classified as being SGE or EGM, but only two have any gender design features.

92.   An electricity distribution and transmission project in Azerbaijan—the project preparatory technical assistance (PPTA) Preparing Multitranche Financing Facility Power Distribution Enhancement Investment Programme—is classified as an EGM project focused on the rehabilitation of distribution lines and substations, and has both organizational and beneficiary-level gender-responsive features. Under its due diligence measures, one target aimed at building the capacity of female energy employees requires that at least 20% of female staff from Azerishiq will be trained in key aspects of distribution network management. There is also a focus on economic empowerment of women, with a requirement that newly recruited customer care jobs under the program will include at least 80% female staff members. Another focus is amplifying women's voices, with a requirement that at least 50% female representation will be ensured in the consultation process during the project implementation period.

93.   In the Kyrgyz Republic, a project aimed at energy sector development and reform, the Uch-Kurgan Hydropower Plant Modernization Project, includes gender design features, such that (i) female engineer teams will be trained to support a new enterprise resource planning system to be installed, and (ii) the project will create a mentoring scheme to create secondment opportunities for female staff in international organizations. There is also an organizational-level focus on publishing sex-disaggregated employment data at all levels of the organization. The project will also emphasize women's economic empowerment and capacity building, with a plan to recruit 10 female engineers for 2 years under the project.

94.   The PPTA Preparing Multitranche Financing Facility Power Distribution Enhancement Investment Programme is classified as an EGM project. It contains some features promoting gender sensitivity that are also transferable to other projects across the CAREC region. In particular, the project seeks to address the gender gap in employment through the identification of

entry points for women. The PPTA update for the project will determine the sex-disaggregated labor profile of the public utility company Azerishiq and suggest ways in which the new jobs created through the investment program can be used to recruit female workers. A target of 20% inclusion of women has also been set for sector development training.[119] The loan program, developed as a result of the PPTA, was categorized as NGE. However, it did had a different effect on new jobs created at Azerishiq by working on provisions for hiring women in customer care positions.

95.   With regard to **amplifying women's voices** through their consultation or inclusion in program design, the program also mandated 50% female representation in project consultations. The specific actions for the inclusion of women identified in the consultations were: (i) informing women of the maintenance shutdown schedule in advance so as to avoid or reduce inconvenience during temporary interruption in power supply for women, who are the primary users of energy at home; (ii) educating women on the use of energy-efficient appliances and lighting equipment at the household level, as they are often the primary energy consumers; (iii) educating women about the benefits of the use of household electrical appliances for reducing time poverty; and (iv) informing and educating women on safety in using electricity and gas in the home.[120]

2.   Gender-Responsive Design Features of Other Funders' Energy Projects

96.   Ten other funders have energy projects in the CAREC 2014–2018 energy portfolio, all of which have a minimum set of integrated gender elements. In all World Bank projects, gender-disaggregated data for beneficiaries, beneficiary satisfaction, and beneficiary feedback are captured.

97.   The GEF-UNDP Green Energy and Small and Medium-Sized Enterprise Development Project in Tajikistan takes an innovative approach to building women's technical capacity and entrepreneurship skills, involving women as green energy consumers as well as entrepreneurs.

98.   The Global Environment Facility (GEF) project by UNDP, and the Nurek Hydropower Rehabilitation Project by the World Bank can also be considered good practice examples of gender mainstreaming in energy initiatives (Box 4 and Box 5).

Box 4: Good Practice on an Energy Project by the United Nations Development Programme

The Global Environment Facility (GEF) has been working with the Ministry of Energy and Water Resources and other relevant government agencies in Tajikistan to support the establishment of Info-Educational Centers on Green Energy in two priority regions. The project will offer training to women interested in establishing green energy small and medium-sized enterprises and energy cooperatives and mobilizing communities in the use of clean energy such as do-it-yourself solar thermal systems, and installation and maintenance of household photovoltaic systems or energy-efficient cook stoves. This activity is based on a recent United Nations Development Programme pilot project in which 15 women were trained to produce their own solar thermal systems based on locally available, affordable, and reliable materials. This experience revealed high demand and potential for such solutions among Tajik women.

Sources: UNDP/GEF. Green Energy and Small and Medium-sized Enterprise Development Project. https://www.tj.undp.org/content/tajikistan/en/home/projects/energy-and-environment/ongoing-projects/UNDP-GEF-Green-Energy-and-SME-Development-Project.html; Global Environment Facility. 2016. GEF Introduction Seminar. https://www.thegef.org/events/gef-introduction-seminar-2016;

---

[119] ADB. 2015. *Initial Poverty and Social Analysis: Preparing MFF Power Distribution Enhancement Investment Programme.* Manila.

[120] ADB. 2016. *Summary Poverty Reduction and Social Analysis: MFF Power Distribution Enhancement Investment Programme.* Manila.

> ### Box 5: Good Practice on an Energy Project by the World Bank
>
> As part of the World Bank–funded Nurek Hydropower Rehabilitation Project in Tajikistan, a social engagement plan was prepared, keeping in mind approaches needed to ensure the engagement of groups susceptible to exclusion (such as women, people with disabilities, and the elderly). In addition, women's questions and complaints related to impacts of the project will be encouraged and monitored. This will be done through the proposed intermediate results indicator on the percentage of registered project-related grievances (disaggregated by gender) responded to within stipulated service standard for such responses.
>
> Source: World Bank. 2017. *Nurek Hydropower Rehabilitation Project Phase I*. Washington, DC.

C. Gender Analysis of CAREC Trade Projects

99.   Of the 11 trade projects assessed, there was only one SGE project: the Mongolia Regional Improvement of Border Services Project, with most of its gender-related activities contributing to reduced time poverty. The project sets a minimum threshold for female employment in the project (20% of unskilled labor). The project also trains customs and border staff, including female staff, on sexually transmitted infections and human trafficking. There are opportunities for cross-project learning, including the requirement of setting a target for the employment of women. There is also an opportunity to translate and share education and awareness materials on sexually transmitted infections and trafficking across the region.

100. All other trade projects were categorized as NGE. The Upgrades of Sanitary and Phytosanitary Measures for Trade Project in Mongolia provides equal opportunities for the capacity building of male and female staff. Hiring women locally and monitoring stall space by gender are part of the project's Social and Development Action Plan. There were no trade projects from other funders.

## CHAPTER IV

MAINSTREAMING GENDER IN CAREC OPERATIONS: ENTRY POINTS

101. While many of the reviewed CAREC projects contain elements that address concerns specific to women or help to increase their participation in economic activity, there is much more that can be done to enhance the scale and scope of gender mainstreaming initiatives. This chapter discusses entry points for gender mainstreaming in CAREC projects, starting with some broad cross-cutting recommendations and then summarizing sector-specific recommendations, using the framework of the new operational clusters set out in the CAREC 2030 strategy. Additional entry points are outlined for the ICT sector, which is a cross-cutting theme over the rest of the CAREC operational clusters. A set of the detailed suggested entry points are included in Annex 1 of the CAREC Gender Strategy 2030.

A. Cross-Cutting Recommendations

1. Conduct Comprehensive Social Inclusion Assessments from the Outset of Any Project

102. The first step toward meaningful gender mainstreaming is to ensure that country-level social inclusion assessments using both qualitative and quantitative methods are conducted. This will enable a better understanding of the specific situations and needs of women and vulnerable groups such as disabled people, the elderly, and the extremely poor. It will also help planners to gain insights into the sociocultural and economic dimensions of gender—vital for adapting and targeting approaches so that, at the very least, interventions do no harm. It is worth noting that gender assessments are currently available for only seven of the 11 CAREC countries. The remaining gender assessments should be conducted in a timely manner to ensure that the specific and differing needs of women in all CAREC countries are taken into account in project development and implementation.

2. Develop a Regional Gender Action Plan

103. Developing a regional gender action plan from the outset, based on findings from the assessment and from other forms of evidence, will facilitate the clear articulation of gender-focused goals and actions aimed at increasing women's inclusion and representation in project outcomes, contributing to women's economic empowerment, reducing their time poverty, and enhancing their role in decision-making—among other goals.

3. Set Minimum Gender Equality and Inclusion Standards

104. The assessment indicates that there is variation in the treatment of issues pertaining to female employment and effective inclusion of female beneficiaries across the CAREC portfolio. The CAREC Program should, therefore, identify minimum standards for application across the program as they pertain to (i) consultation of female beneficiaries, (ii) access to training opportunities for women, (iii) access to employment opportunities for women, and (iv) the quality

of employment to prevent wage discrimination. There are examples of good practices in several projects that can be mainstreamed. Minimum targets for female employment should be defined (some CAREC projects use the baseline of 20%). Where the local context allows for higher targets, the development of more ambitious localized targets should be encouraged, while broadening the focus to include the level and quality of opportunity available for women, in addition to fulfilling employment targets.

B. Sector-Specific Recommendations

1.   Economic and Financial Stability Cluster

105. Strengthening economic and financial stability for women involves introducing measures that will, at a minimum, provide access to jobs, improve job skills, increase financial inclusion, and support entrepreneurship. While some CAREC projects contain elements that indirectly address these concerns, there are additional entry points that can be explored.

106. Strategic directions for mainstreaming gender into this cluster include generating economic opportunities for women through policies and strategies that include setting targets for the employment of women—including in nontraditional jobs and management—and creating employment standards that promote decent work for all. This also means creating an enabling environment for female entrepreneurs, including the promotion of improved financial access, and building women's and girls' capacity in STEM subjects and ICT to promote their access to emerging areas of employment in CAREC countries. It is vital to inform these strategies with relevant qualitative and quantitative evidence gathered through consultative processes with female and male beneficiaries, financial providers and employers, and surveys. Establishing networks for businesswomen's associations from all 11 CAREC countries will also help strengthen cooperation and promote investment opportunities across the region.

107. Measures are needed to promote policy dialogue at regional and cross-country levels. These could include the sharing of counter-cyclical policy initiatives that include the provision of budgetary support to social infrastructure (for example, for health and education) and to MSMEs headed by women.

108. Gender-responsive adjustments in the banking sector are required. These should include better coordinated banking regulations to improve financial inclusion for women and other marginalized groups, supported by regional financial models that promote female entrepreneurship. Private sector actors should strengthen their commitment to women's economic empowerment through gender-responsive actions that include cross-border investments in agribusiness and tourism.

2.   Trade, Tourism, and Economic Corridors Cluster

109. Supporting trade, tourism, and economic corridors in a gender-sensitive manner will help to create new opportunities for women as business owners and investors. Supporting women's entrepreneurship and investment will improve the quality and type of work available for women in the sector. Many CAREC projects falling under this operational cluster have some elements specifically addressing women's concerns to support gender mainstreaming. These efforts can be strengthened and their scale expanded and replicated across the CAREC portfolio.

a.   Trade

110.   In order to boost gender inclusiveness across all aspects of trade and create an enabling environment for the economic empowerment of both female entrepreneurs and informal cross-border traders, it is vital to revise both national and regional trade policies to include gender-responsive measures. For example, preferential conditions and tariffs could be introduced for female traders, including the reduction of the barriers faced by many female cross-border traders. Finance policies should promote incentives for the private sector and female-owned MSMEs, and government procurement policies should support the sourcing of goods and services from female-led enterprises. Additionally, agricultural policies should enable female farmers to enter and benefit from gender-equitable value chains.

111.   Any new or revised policies should be informed through consultations with female traders to understand their specific needs and the constraints they face. Clear information on any changes should be provided and effectively disseminated to female traders. The success of policies and processes in enabling women's economic empowerment should be measured by setting and mapping progress against target numbers of female traders nationally and regionally, across CAREC countries.

112.   Regional trading policies must ensure that goods have been produced under safe working conditions, free from exploitation. Information and appropriate training should be provided for police, border staff, and customs officials to reduce the risk of trafficking, sexual exploitation, gender-based violence, and sexual harassment. Information on preventing sexually transmitted diseases such as HIV/AIDS should also be available for predominantly male workers transporting goods, such as lorry drivers. It is also important to mitigate against potentially negative impacts of formalizing border trade, such as harassment or extortion by market and trade officials who may take advantage of female traders' often limited access to information on market rules.[121]

b.   Tourism

113.   It is vital to ensure women have equal access to information about tourism-related jobs, but regional and cross-country guidelines should be developed to ensure that recruitment is based on skills and experience rather than on physical appearance, and that women receive gender-equitable pay and have equal access to opportunities such as on-the-job training.

114.   It is vital to involve women and men from local communities in the planning, development, and running of tourist attractions and related services to ensure they benefit directly from these initiatives and that profits go back into the community.

115.   Appropriate and proportionate measures must also be taken to address and minimize the risks of sexual exploitation, sexual abuse, and trafficking that are often associated with tourism. Taking these issues seriously means ensuring zero tolerance is written into law and implemented by police, border guards, tourist industry leaders, and national and local governments. It also means providing region-wide as well as country-specific targeted information

---

[121]   K. Higgins. 2012. *Gender Dimensions of Trade Facilitation and Logistics: A Guidance Note.* World Bank International Trade Department. http://siteresources.worldbank.org/INTRANETTRADE/Resources/Pubs/Gender_Dimensions_Trade_Facilitation_Logistics_ Higgins_electronic.pdf (20/3/20).

and training for those responsible for implementing anti-trafficking, sexual exploitation, and sexual abuse legislation in the context of tourism.

c.   Economic Corridors

116.   The development of CAREC economic corridors offers great scope for the creation of jobs and promotion of entrepreneurship. These projects require close coordination among different stakeholders, such as governments and the private sector; and multidisciplinary approaches are necessary. Economic corridors such as the Almaty-Bishkek Economic Corridor and the Trilateral Economic Corridor connecting Kazakhstan, Uzbekistan, and Tajikistan could be used to increase women's participation in all related activities such as cross-border trade, tourism and related services, regional value chains, urban planning, knowledge sharing, and training events.

3.   Infrastructure and Economic Connectivity Cluster

a.   Transport

117.   It is vital to ensure public transport services are convenient, accessible, and safe for all women and children. This means ensuring the provision of affordable services for women and families to accommodate women's specific travel patterns; ensuring designs are sensitive to gender-differentiated needs—for example, with space for baby carriages and separate sections or carriages and ticket offices for women, where this would increase their accessibility.

118.   It is particularly important to integrate measures that address and reduce the risk of sexual and other forms of harassment for women using public transport, given the extent to which this has been reported as a growing problem in many CAREC countries. This means ensuring transport service providers receive training in protecting women from sexual harassment, introducing a zero-tolerance policy for any form of sexual harassment, whether verbal or physical, and improving systems for reporting harassment in secure ways. It also means launching information campaigns for transport users and the public to raise awareness about these issues and encourage reporting of perpetrators.

119.   At the regional and country-cluster level, networks should be created to link transport providers, law enforcement agencies, medical professions, and nongovernment organizations in order to monitor safety provisions and to safeguard female transport users through the provision of effective reporting and tracking systems.

120.   It is imperative to understand the specific needs of women and men when designing both main and feeder roads to ensure everyone can access and benefit from them fully and safely. Adequate lighting must be provided along routes to bus stops and local villages to make women and other vulnerable groups visible to oncoming traffic and to make them less susceptible to threats such as theft or sexual harassment.[122] The provision of suitable walkways, pedestrian bridges, and bus shelters is also vital to ensure accessibility, comfort, and safety (footnote 56). Mandatory road safety measures and clear signage are vital for both (often male) drivers and pedestrians in CAREC countries. Additionally, accessible gender-sensitive amenities, such as disabled accessible toilets and service stops, must be provided for both women and men on major transport routes.

---

[122] Footnote 20.

121. Regional and national-level policies and guidelines should be established to increase employment opportunities for women in transport, going beyond the stereotypical roles in administration and encouraging their application for technical and managerial roles in road and rail transport, aviation, and logistics. This means ensuring that application processes for transport firms are gender-sensitive and transparent, not discriminating on the grounds of gender. It also means encouraging girls to study STEM subjects that will prepare them for technical roles, as well as providing on-the-job training and providing regional and country-cluster-level training programs for those already working in transport or who aspire to do so. Setting targets for female employees and managers in the transport sector will enable progress in women's economic empowerment to be tracked.

b.   Energy

122. It is vital for energy provision to take into account women's needs and to make sure, above all, that they have access to affordable, targeted services. This means ensuring that all aspects of energy service design are grounded in gender-sensitive evidence gathered through consultative processes and surveys. To ensure the poorest and most vulnerable people can access clean energy supplies, companies and governments should explore the provision of free or affordable credit for customers who may be unable to afford regular tariffs. At national and regional levels, energy policies should promote social and environmental impacts, with a focus on reducing domestic energy costs to increase access for poorer households—including those households that are headed by women—and providing low-cost carbon-neutral energy options.

123. National and regional information systems should be created or improved to generate sex-disaggregated data on issues such as accessibility, affordability, and income generation to inform transport and energy planning. Learning among CAREC countries must also be enabled, for example, through regional exchanges between government ministries, private sector companies, female energy sector professionals, and nongovernment organizations.

124. The energy sector could provide a useful source of employment for women, particularly in the growing sustainable energy market. For example, economic opportunities can be created for women in the emerging green energy sector by training them in technology and sales for renewable energy products such as solar lamps.[123] It is also important to create opportunities for women to take up technical and professional posts with energy suppliers. At the regional and cross-country levels, partnerships should be developed between energy suppliers, universities, and technical and vocational education and training (TVET) institutions to provide professional development for women in energy-related operations and maintenance.

4.   Agriculture and Water Cluster

a.   Agriculture

125. Closing the gender gap in agriculture requires multiple actions at the policy and practical levels. This means developing both regional and country-level approaches to promote gender-equitable land ownership and access. It also means ensuring women have equal access to credit, agricultural extension services, and digital technologies such as

---

[123] In Pakistan, ACTED launched a pilot project to promote sustainable solutions for women's empowerment, providing technical training in solar energy. With support from the ADB, ACTED trained 54 women in Multan, Punjab, as solar technicians. Footnote 105.

mobile phones and apps connecting them to market pricing information and potential buyers. Intercountry capacity development should also be created for women farmers on new agricultural practices and technologies.

126. Intercountry agricultural value chain channels should be created for female producers and agricultural entrepreneurs, supported by the development of digital platforms and apps to promote gender-sensitive cross-border agricultural trade.

b.   Water

127.   Women are often the primary beneficiaries of water-related infrastructure, so it is vital to ensure their specific needs are met and their time poverty reduced by engaging them in the design process through grassroots consultations. Effective mechanisms must also be established for registering and responding to any questions or grievances related to water supply.

128.   Women must be active participants in regional mechanisms for transboundary water resource management. They must also be equally represented in cross-country or regional-level pandemic responses to address impacts on food and water security and water and sanitation infrastructure.

129.   The growing water sector in many CAREC countries is also a potential source of well-paid employment for women, not only in administrative but also in technical and managerial roles. This means actively recruiting women into technical and managerial roles in the water sector and providing on-the-job training.

5.   Human Development

a.   Education

130.   A number of CAREC projects undertake site-specific education activities aimed at awareness-raising among staff and construction workers on issues such as sexual harassment, violence against women, HIV/AIDS, and human trafficking. While these measures are designed to improve living and working conditions in CAREC project areas, and while women benefit indirectly from improved knowledge on these issues, there is scope to expand the range of education initiatives to benefit women directly, including by training them to take up jobs and participate in local economies that will spring up in CAREC project areas.

131.   CAREC should actively promote better alignment of women's educational choices with employment opportunities nationally and across the CAREC region. Strategies at the regional and intercountry levels could include partnering with national and regional TVET providers to offer courses including on digital platforms—in sectors relevant for CAREC project areas, with emphasis on training women in nontraditional skills such as plumbing, carpentry, electrical work, and machine operation. CAREC should also promote girls and women in STEM subjects to help offset the risks of early dropout. CAREC could work with national governments to create clear messaging on the importance of educating girls in certain countries.

132.   Steps should be taken at the regional and country levels to increase women's representation in management and decision-making of schools and universities, including TVET institutions.

b. Health

133. A regional approach to strengthen surveillance systems and monitoring capabilities across borders for control of communicable and noncommunicable diseases and improve access of women and men to quality and more affordable services should be sought. CAREC can also add enormous value by exploring and sharing knowledge on digital solutions such as tele-health and e-health services in the remote areas that are so poorly served in many CAREC countries.

134. Cross-country exchange of affordable, innovative technologies for maternal health care and the provision of services to remote, underserved areas should be encouraged.

6. Information and Communication Technology

135. ICT is a cross-cutting consideration for all CAREC clusters and, therefore, needs to be taken into account in all planning and implementation. CAREC can help close the digital gender divide by supporting capacity building in ICT for women and girls of all ages, including both students and teachers in schools and higher education institutions in CAREC countries. Regional or intercountry partnerships should be created with private sector digital providers to support the provision of internet access to poor households, particularly those in remote and rural areas. Regional networks to share gender-sensitive practices for enhancing women's access to ICT and increasing their opportunities in information technology–related employment could also be established.

LIST OF CAREC PROJECTS, 2014–2018 ANALYZED FOR THIS ASSESSMENT

I. Transport Sector

	Project Name	Country	Funder	Project Type	Description	Gender Classification
1	East–West Highway (Kevi–Ubisa Section) Improvement Project	Georgia	ADB	Road transport (nonurban)	Improving the Khevi–Ubisa section and operations and maintenance of the road network, as well as road safety	EGM
2	North–South Corridor (Kvesheti–Kobi) Road Project	Georgia	ADB	Road transport (nonurban)	Improving connectivity and safety along the North–South Corridor	EGM
3	Preparing the North–South Corridor (Kvesheti–Kobi) Road Project	Georgia	ADB	Road transport (nonurban)	TRTA to assist the Government of Georgia with project preparation	EGM
4	CAREC Corridors 2, 3, and 5 (Obigarm–Nurobod) Road Project	Tajikistan	ADB	Road transport (nonurban)	Improving connectivity, safety and women's access to economic opportunities along the Obigarm–Nurobod road	EGM
5	Preparing CAREC Corridors 2, 3, and 5 (Obigarm–Nurobod) Road Project	Tajikistan	ADB	Road transport (nonurban)	TRTA to help the government of Tajikistan with project preparation	EGM
6	Preparing the CAREC 2,3, and 6 (Turkmenabat–Mary–Ashgabat–Turkmenbashi) Railway Modernization Project	Turkmenistan	ADB	Rail transport	The Government of Turkmenistan and the Ministry of Railway Transport requested assistance from ADB for a program to modernize railways in Turkmenistan, between Turkmenabat, Mary, Ashgabat, and Turkmenbashi.	EGM
7	Preparing CAREC Corridors 1 and 3 (Bishkek Northern Bypass) Road Project	Kyrgyz Republic	ADB	Road transport (nonurban)	TRTA to help the government prepare the road reconstruction project, design the reform program for road safety, and design the vocational education project	EGM
8	MFF: Transport Network Development Investment Program, Tranche 4	Afghanistan	ADB	Road transport (nonurban)	Reconstruction of the remaining 108 km gap from Beharak to Eshkashim in the envisaged northeastern corridor	EGM

continued on next page

Transport Sector *continued*

	Project Name	Country	Funder	Project Type	Description	Gender Classification
9	CAREC Corridors 1 and 3 Connector Road Project (Phase 2) Additional Financing	Kyrgyz Republic	ADB	Road transport (nonurban)	Connecting two major CAREC regional corridors by rehabilitating a crucial connector road, part of the North–South Alternate Corridor, which is a priority in the National Sustainable Development Strategy	SGE
10	CAREC Corridors 1 and 3 Connector Road Project	Kyrgyz Republic	ADB	Road transport (nonurban)	Connecting two major CAREC regional corridors by rehabilitating a crucial connector road, part of the North–South Alternate Corridor	SGE
11	CAREC Corridors 1 and 3 Connector Road Project Design Advance	Kyrgyz Republic	ADB	Road transport (nonurban)	The project design advance aimed to fund (i) the engineering consultant recruited to prepare the detailed design and advance procurement actions of the project, and (ii) the financial audit firm required for auditing the use of the project design advance.	SGE
12	CAREC Corridors 1 and 3 Connector Road Project	Kyrgyz Republic	ADB	Road transport (nonurban)	PPTA to identify, formulate, and prepare an ensuing loan and/or grant for the CAREC Corridors 1 and 3 Connector Road. The main outcome of the PPTA was to prepare a feasibility study suitable for ADB financing.	SGE
13	CAREC Corridors 2, 5, and 6 (Dushanbe–Kurgonteppa) Road Project Additional Financing	Tajikistan	ADB	Road transport (nonurban)	Additional financing to support an increase in the scope of the current project by constructing a 40-km road section connecting Chashmasoron to Kurgonteppa in Khatlon Province, improving safety on priority sections of the national highway network, and strengthening institutional capacity of the Ministry of Transport	SGE
14	CAREC Corridors 2, 5, and 6 (Dushanbe–Kurgonteppa) Road Project	Tajikistan	ADB	Road transport (nonurban)	Improving connectivity between the capital of Dushanbe and Kurgonteppa, which are two major cities and economic hubs in Tajikistan	SGE
15	CAREC Corridors 2, 5, and 6 (Dushanbe–Kurgonteppa) Road Project (Supplementary)	Tajikistan	ADB	Road transport (nonurban)	PPTA to help identify, formulate, and prepare a loan and/or grant for a 20-km section of the Dushanbe to Kurgonteppa road, which forms part of CAREC Corridors 2, 5, and 6	SGE
16	Support to the Advisory Group on Railway Sector Development	Afghanistan	ADB	Rail transport	TA to develop road map for the development of Afghanistan's railway subsector	SGE
17	Qaisar–Dari Bum Road Project	Afghanistan	ADB	Road transport (nonurban)	Helping the government to promote economic and social development and reduce poverty by rehabilitating the primary road network damaged during 2 decades of conflict and neglect	SGE
18	Rail Sector Development Program	Azerbaijan	ADB	Rail transport (nonurban)	Providing project financing for the rehabilitation of the track and structure of the Sumgayit–Yalama rail line—a key link in the North–South Railway Corridor within CAREC	SGE

continued on next page

Transport Sector *continued*

	Project Name	Country	Funder	Project Type	Description	Gender Classification
19	Railway Sector Development Program	Azerbaijan	ADB	Rail transport (nonurban)	PPTA to prepare (i) a comprehensive policy matrix for the policy-based loan—covering institutional changes at ADY and in the railways sector, financial restructuring at ADY, a sector development plan, and other policy areas; (ii) a feasibility study for track renewal and a computerized freight operation system; and (iii) ADB loan processing documents	SGE
20	Railway Efficiency Improvement Project	Uzbekistan	ADB	Rail transport (nonurban)	TA to help the Government of Uzbekistan prepare the project, develop the appropriate institutional conditions to allow the sound development of the railway sector in future years, and develop the capacity to implement the ensuing project	SGE
21	CAREC Corridor 2 (Pap–Namangan–Andijan) Railway Electrification Project	Uzbekistan	ADB	Rail transport (nonurban)	Electrification of the missing 145.1 km of non-electrified track linking major cities in the populous Fergana Valley with Tashkent	SGE
22	Preparation of CAREC Corridor 2 (Pap–Namangan–Andijan) Railway Electrification Project	Uzbekistan	ADB	Rail transport (nonurban)	PPTA to improve the feasibility study and produce mutually agreed design and implementation arrangements suitable for ADB financing, including pre-implementation works for the project	SGE
23	CAREC Corridors 1 and 6 Connector (Aktobe–Makat) Reconstruction Project	Kazakhstan	ADB	Road transport (nonurban)	Reconstruction of a road section of 299 km between the capitals and administration centers of Aktobe and Atyrau provinces in western Kazakhstan, and introduction of key features of a transport information system	SGE
24	CAREC Corridors 1 and 6 Connector Road (Aktobe–Makat) Improvement Project	Kazakhstan	ADB	Road transport (nonurban)	PPTA in which the Committee on Roads engaged the state design institute Kostanay Dorproject to carry out a detailed engineering design	SGE
25	CAREC Corridors 1 and 6 Connector Road (Aktobe–Makat) Improvement Project (Supplementary)	Kazakhstan	ADB	Road transport (nonurban)	No description available	SGE
26	Enabling Economic Corridors through Sustainable Transport Sector Development	Pakistan	ADB	Transport policies (institutional development)	Improving the capacity of the Government of Pakistan to develop and manage its transport system in a coordinated, efficient, safe, and sustainable manner	SGE
27	Regional Road Development and Maintenance Project	Mongolia	ADB	Road transport (nonurban)	Rehabilitating and enhancing the safety of important regional road corridor sections between Ulaanbaatar and Altanbulag	EGM

continued on next page

Transport Sector *continued*

	Project Name	Country	Funder	Project Type	Description	Gender Classification
28	Regional Road Development and Maintenance Project	Mongolia	ADB	Road Transport (nonurban)—transport policies and institutional development	PPTA to help the Government of Mongolia design the Regional Road Development and Maintenance Project financing	SGE
29	MFF: Western Regional Road Corridor Development Program Tranche 2	Mongolia	ADB	Road transport (nonurban)	Supporting the development of a transport corridor that links Mongolia to the Russian Federation in the north and the People's Republic of China in the south	SGE
30	Third Phase of the Central Asia Regional Links Program	Kyrgyz Republic	World Bank	Road transport and tourism development	Regional Connections, Associated Facilities and Equipment in Issyk–Kul Oblast, including rehabilitation of 52 km of road section in Issyk–Kul Oblast; sustainable tourism development in Issyk–Kul Oblast and development of a sustainable tourism strategy and masterplan; and support for the development of community–based geo-parks	N/A
31	Reconstruction of Atyrau–Astrakhan Road (CAREC Corridors 6A) Project	Kazakhstan	Islamic Development Bank	Road transport (nonurban)	No description available	N/A
32	Third Highway Project (additional financing)	Azerbaijan	World Bank	Road transport (nonurban)	Contributing to a more efficient and safer Baku–Shamakhi road and higher quality road services as part of the upgrading to motorway standards and improving the management of the nascent motorway network	N/A
33	Pap–Angren Railway	Uzbekistan	World Bank	Rail transport (nonurban)	Reducing transport costs and increasing transport capacity and reliability through the construction of a rail link between the Uzbek part of the Ferghana Valley and the rest of Uzbekistan	N/A
34	Olzha Phase III Loan	Kazakhstan	EBRD	Rail transport	Secured loan to JSC Olzha, a private operator of freight wagons in Kazakhstan, with proceeds of the loan to be used for acquisition of new freight railcars	N/A
35	Olzha Loan Extension	Kazakhstan	EBRD	Rail transport	Secured loan to JSC Olzha, to be used for the acquisition of new freight railcars and one shunting locomotive	N/A
36	Astana Airport Rehabilitation	Kazakhstan	EBRD	Air transport	Financing the rehabilitation of the runway, taxiways, and apron, and upgrade of lighting navigational aids at Astana Airport as part of the airport modernization project	N/A
37	Third CAREC Corridor Road Investment Program	Uzbekistan	ADB	Road transport (nonurban)	PPTA to carry out due diligence and prepare a comprehensive design under the Third CAREC Corridor 2 Road Investment Program	NGE

continued on next page

Transport Sector *continued*

	Project Name	Country	Funder	Project Type	Description	Gender Classification
38	CAREC Corridor 3 (Bishkek–Osh) Road Improvement Project Phase 4	Kyrgyz Republic	ADB	Road transport (nonurban)	TA to identify, formulate, and prepare an ensuing loan and/or grant for the CAREC Corridor 3 (Bishkek–Osh Road) Improvement Project, Phase 4	NGE
39	Enhancing Road Safety for Central Asia Regional Economic Cooperation Member Countries, Supplementary	Regional	ADB	Road transport (nonurban)	TA on road safety intended to reduce the burden associated with road collisions in CAREC member countries	NGE
40	MFF: CAREC Corridor Development Investment Program Tranche 1	Pakistan	ADB	Road transport (nonurban)	MFF aimed at enhancing regional connectivity and trade in the CAREC corridors in Pakistan by improving the efficiency of road traffic along the CAREC corridors	NGE
41	Road Asset Management Project Additional Financing	Afghanistan	ADB	Road transport (nonurban)	Road asset management project to finance priority maintenance works for part of Afghanistan's regional highway sections from Kabul to Ghazni and from Kabul to Jalalabad, which are the economic lifeline of the country's eastern region	NGE
42	Railway Sector Development Program (Supplementary)	Azerbaijan	ADB	Rail transport (nonurban)	Transforming ADY into a profitable company and to improve railway service delivery through (i) railway sector and corporate reforms and ADY financial restructuring; and (ii) improvements to railway infrastructure, particularly along the north–south railway corridor	NGE
43	Batumi Bypass Road Project	Georgia	ADB	Road transport (nonurban)	Constructing a new two–lane bypass road of 16.2 km skirting Batumi; and contracting out routine and periodic maintenance work for about 200 km of international roads combined with connecting secondary roads	NGE
44	CAREC Knowledge–Sharing and Services in Transport Facilitation, Supplementary	Regional	ADB	Transport policies and institutional development	TA acts as a vehicle for generation, management, and dissemination of knowledge aimed at strengthening the implementation of the CAREC Transport and Trade Facilitation Strategy 2020	NGE
45	Road Asset Management Project	Afghanistan	ADB	Road transport (nonurban)	The grant finances priority maintenance works for part of Afghanistan's regional highway sections from Kabul to Ghazni and from Kabul to Jalalabad, which are the economic lifeline of the country's eastern region	NGE
46	Preparation of CAREC Corridors 5 and 6 (Salang Corridor)	Afghanistan	ADB	Road transport (nonurban)	Upgrading the Salang Corridor	NGE
47	CAREC Railway Connectivity Program	Pakistan	ADB	Rail transport (nonurban)	PPTA to (i) develop an MFF and tranche projects bankable by ADB loan; and (ii) conduct due diligence for technical, economic, financial, social, and environmental viability of the first tranche project and prepare required due diligence documents	NGE

continued on next page

Transport Sector *continued*

	Project Name	Country	Funder	Project Type	Description	Gender Classification
48	Development of Road Safety Policy and Action Plan for Mongolia	Mongolia	ADB	Transport policies and institutional development	Supporting the Government of Mongolia to improve its road safety management capacity to reduce accident levels and related fatalities	NGE
49	Railway Sector Development Program	Azerbaijan	ADB	Rail transport (nonurban)	Transforming ADY into a profitable company and improving railway service delivery through (i) railway sector and corporate reforms and ADY financial restructuring; and (ii) improvements to railway infrastructure, particularly along the north–south railway corridor	NGE
50	National Motorway M-4 Gojra–Shorkot–Khanewal Section Project (Additional Financing)	Pakistan	ADB	Transport policies and institutional development	Supporting an increase in the scope of the current project by constructing a 64-km four-lane, access-controlled motorway connecting Shorkot and Khanewal in Punjab Province	NGE
51	CAREC Knowledge–Sharing and Services in Transport Facilitation	Regional	ADB	Transport policies and institutional development	TA acts as a vehicle for generation, management, and dissemination of knowledge aimed at strengthening the implementation of the CAREC Transport and Trade Facilitation Strategy 2020	NGE
52	MFF: Second CAREC Corridor 2 Road Investment Program Tranche 3	Uzbekistan	ADB	Road transport (nonurban)	Improving road connectivity, efficiency of transport system, and effectiveness of management for the Uzbekistan sections of the CAREC Corridor 2 Road	NGE
53	CAREC Regional Improving Border Services Project	Pakistan	ADB	Multimodal logistics	Improving border–crossing point infrastructure and facility at Torkham, Chaman, and Wagha to the standard that meets users' demand for quality border–crossing services, and establishing a border point management regime and enhance knowledge and skills of border point operating agencies	NGE
54	National Motorway M-4 Gojra–Shorkot Section Project	Pakistan	ADB	Road transport (nonurban)	Supporting an increase in the scope of the current project by constructing a 64-km four-lane, access-controlled motorway connecting Shorkot and Khanewal in Punjab Province	NGE
55	Third CAREC Corridor Road Investment Program	Uzbekistan	ADB	Road transport (nonurban)	PPTA to carry out due diligence and prepare a comprehensive design under the Third CAREC Corridor 2 Road Investment Program	NGE
56	CAREC Corridor Development Investment Program	Pakistan	ADB	Road transport (nonurban)	TA to design MFF to assist the government in improving the CAREC corridors to serve the needs of surrounding countries to be interconnected through Pakistan and thereby acting as a regional hub to promote regional integration and intra– and inter–regional trade	NGE

continued on next page

Transport Sector *continued*

	Project Name	Country	Funder	Project Type	Description	Gender Classification
57	CAREC Knowledge–Sharing and Services in Transport and Transport Facilitation	Regional	ADB	Transport policies and institutional development	TA acts as a vehicle for generation, management, and dissemination of knowledge aimed at strengthening the implementation of the CAREC Transport and Trade Facilitation Strategy 2020	NGE
58	CAREC Transport Corridor 1 (Bishkek–Torugart Road) Project 3 (Additional Financing)	Kyrgyz Republic	ADB	Road transport (nonurban)	Improving the last 60 km bottleneck section of CAREC Corridor 1 (Bishkek–Torugart Road), with a goal of fostering regional trade between the Kyrgyz Republic and the PRC and improving mobility for people in Naryn Province, where poverty is widespread	NGE
59	MFF: National Trade Corridor Highway Investment Program, Tranche 3	Pakistan	ADB	Road transport (nonurban)	Project 3 (E35: Hasanabdal–Havelian Expressway Package–3) was part of the National Trade Corridor and CAREC Corridor 5. E–35 connects the existing Islamabad–Peshawar Motorway M1 near Hasanabdal–Havelian Expressway near Abbotabad.	NGE
60	Enhancing Road Safety for Central Asia Regional Economic Cooperation Member Countries	Regional	ADB	Road transport (nonurban)	TA on road safety intended to reduce the burden associated with road collisions in CAREC member countries	NGE
61	MFF: Second Road Network Development Program Tranche 2	Azerbaijan	ADB	Road transport (nonurban); transport policies and institutional development	Developing Jalilabad to Shorsulu motorway section and provide sector capacity development	NGE
62	Transport Sector Master Plan Update	Afghanistan	ADB	Transport policies and institutional development	TA to study proposed new investment projects as well as both maintenance activities and soft issues such as demand management, pricing, and transport sector reforms	NGE
63	MFF: National Trade Corridor Highway Investment Program Tranche 2	Pakistan	ADB	Road transport (nonurban)	The Project 2 (E35: Hasanabdal–Havelian Expressway) was part of the National Trade Corridor and CAREC Corridor 5. It connects the existing Islamabad–Peshawar Motorway M1 near Hasanabdal–Havelian Expressway near Abbotabad	NGE
64	MFF: Road Network Development Program Tranche 4	Azerbaijan	ADB	Road transport (nonurban)	Reconstructing four bridges that were in very poor condition and rehabilitating 30 km of local roads in the Ganja–Qazax region	NGE

II. Energy Sector

	Project Name	Country	Funder	Project Type	Description	Gender Classification
65	MFF Power Distribution Enhancement Investment Program	Azerbaijan	ADB	Electricity transmission and distribution	Supporting the government's efforts in providing reliable and efficient power supply to meet its growing energy needs for inclusive development, especially in secondary cities and rural areas	SGE
66	Preparing MFF Power Distribution Enhancement Investment Program	Azerbaijan	ADB	Electricity transmission and distribution; energy efficiency and conservation	The project aims to improve efficiency of the power distribution subsector in Azerbaijan through rehabilitation and expansion of an aged power distribution network. It will (i) improve power supply reliability, (ii) reduce distribution network losses, (iii) improve customer service efficiency and quality, (iv) improve operational and financial performance of the distribution company, and (v) promote corporate reform and institutional development in the distribution subsector.	EGM
67	Uch–Kurgan Hydropower Plant Modernization	Kyrgyz Republic	ADB	Energy efficiency and conservation; energy sector development and institutional reform; large hydropower generation	Replacing aging electrical and mechanical equipment for power generation and transmission at the Uch–Kurgan HPP in the Naryn River cascade and undertaking silt and sedimentation removal	SGE
68	Uch–Kurgan Hydropower Plant Modernization	Kyrgyz Republic	ADB	Large hydropower generation	PPTA to (i) review the technical, environmental, economic, and financial viability of the project and ascertain the project rationale, scope, cost, schedule, implementation arrangements, risks, and mitigation measures; (ii) ensure the compliance with ADB's safeguard policy statement (2009) and identify mitigation measures and institutional strengthening; and (iii) assist the project executing agency in advance contracting for the ensuing project	SGE
69	Leapfrogging of Clean Technology in CAREC Countries through Market Transformation	Regional	ADB	Energy efficiency and conservation	TA aimed at building capacities through targeted training, demonstration projects, and knowledge products	SGE

continued on next page

Energy Sector *continued*

	Project Name	Country	Funder	Project Type	Description	Gender Classification
70	Access to Electricity with New Off-Grid Solar Technology	Regional	ADB	Energy sector development and institutional reform	TA to demonstrate the technical and financial viability of this new technology combination in the CAREC region, and enable the off-grid community to move from basic lighting to a range of basic battery-operated appliances using larger solar panels and long-life lithium-ion batteries	SGE
71	Green Energy and Small and Medium-Sized Enterprise Development Project	Tajikistan	GEF		TA to identify, support, and promote scalable, private sector-led business models for provision of affordable and sustainable energy products and services for Tajikistan's rural population	N/A
72	Energy Efficiency Facility for Industrial Enterprises, Phase 3	Uzbekistan	World Bank		Improving energy efficiency in industrial enterprises by designing and establishing a financing mechanism for energy-saving investments	N/A
73	Energy Efficiency Facility for Industrial Enterprises, Phase 3	Uzbekistan	World Bank		Improving energy efficiency in industrial enterprises by designing and establishing a financing mechanism for energy-saving investments	N/A
74	District Heating Energy Efficiency Project	Uzbekistan	World Bank		Improve the efficiency and quality of heating and hot water services in selected cities within Uzbekistan	N/A
75	Heat Supply Improvement Project	Kyrgyz Republic	World Bank		Improving the efficiency and quality of heating in selected project areas	N/A
76	Nurek Hydropower Rehabilitation Project, Phase 1	Tajikistan	World Bank		The objectives of the first phase of Nurek Hydropower Rehabilitation Project for Tajikistan were to (i) rehabilitate and restore the generating capacity of three power generating units of Nurek HPP, (ii) improve their efficiency, and (iii) strengthen the safety of the Nurek dam.	N/A
77	Modernization and Upgrade of Transmission Substations	Uzbekistan	World Bank		Improving the technical efficiency and reliability of the power transmission networks in Uzbekistan	N/A
78	Oshelectro Rehabilitation Project	Kyrgyz Republic	EBRD		JSC Oshelectro applied for a loan toward financing the rehabilitation and modernization of low- and medium-voltage distribution networks to reduce distribution network losses, increase energy efficiency, and improve quality of supply	N/A
79	Electricity Supply Accountability and Reliability Improvement Project	Kyrgyz Republic	World Bank		Improving the reliability of the electricity supply in the capital city of Bishkek, as well as the Chui and Talas regions—an area served by the state-owned power distribution company Severelectro JSC—and to strengthen the governance of Severelectro's operations	N/A

continued on next page

Energy Sector *continued*

	Project Name	Country	Funder	Project Type	Description	Gender Classification
80	Europe and the CIS Sustainable Energy for All (SE4ALL) Initiative	Regional	UNDP		Action-focused global network supported by partner organizations from governments, national and international organizations, businesses, and civil society organizations, with a regional initiative covering Kazakhstan, the Kyrgyz Republic, Tajikistan, Turkmenistan, and Uzbekistan	N/A
81	Reconnection to the Central Asian Power System	Tajikistan	ADB	Electricity transmission and distribution	Project to (i) install modern relays, circuit breakers, instrumental transformers and ancillary equipment and systems at eight 220 kV and two 500 kV interconnection points; (ii) establish two new 500 kV interconnections; and (iii) provide capacity building to Barki Tojik staff in reliability of parallel operations	NGE
82	National Power Grid Strengthening Project	Turkmenistan	ADB	Electricity transmission and distribution	Project to cover four of the five regions of Turkmenistan, and help establish an interconnected national transmission grid to improve reliability and energy efficiency of the network	NGE
83	Regional Cooperation and Renewable Energy Integration to the Grid	Regional	ADB	Electricity transmission and distribution—solar renewable energy generation—solar, wind	The proposed knowledge and support TA will help Afghanistan, Kazakhstan, the Kyrgyz Republic, Pakistan, Tajikistan, Turkmenistan, and Uzbekistan increase intermittent renewable energy generation (solar and wind power) by providing training to transmission grid operators on modernized control techniques to address renewable energy intermittency and by analyzing regional cooperation arrangement options.	NGE
84	MFF: Energy Supply Improvement Investment Program, Tranche 2	Afghanistan	ADB	Electricity transmission and distribution	Expand power imports from Turkmenistan through an asynchronous power interconnection, establish a unified power grid in Afghanistan, and extend the power grid into central Afghanistan	NGE
85	Energy Development, 2014–2023 (Supplementary)	Afghanistan	ADB	Electricity transmission and distribution; energy sector development and institutional reform	Expand power imports from Turkmenistan through an asynchronous power interconnection, establish a unified power grid in Afghanistan, and extend the power grid into central Afghanistan	NGE
86	Toktogul Rehabilitation Phase 3 Project	Kyrgyz Republic	ADB	Energy efficiency and conservation; energy sector development and institutional reform; large hydropower generation	Completing the rehabilitation of the Toktogul HPP by replacing the two remaining turbine-generator units and refurbishing the civil structures of Toktogul dam, overhauling the dam monitoring systems at five dams along the Naryn cascade, educating the public on sector reforms, conducting corporate financial audits, and implementing a management modernization program for the power generation company	NGE

continued on next page

Energy Sector *continued*

	Project Name	Country	Funder	Project Type	Description	Gender Classification
87	MFF: Energy Supply Improvement Program, Tranche 1	Afghanistan	ADB	Electricity transmission and distribution—energy utility services	The subprojects proposed for financing under the requested PFR were (i) 500 kV transmission line from Sheberghan to Dashte Alwan, (ii) 220 kV transmission line from Andkhoy to Sheberghan, (iii) project preparation facility for future energy projects and provision of analytical consulting services, and (iv) program supervision and implementation consultancy.	NGE
88	Renewable Energy Development	Afghanistan	ADB	Energy sector development and institutional reform	TA to increase the share of renewable energy in Afghanistan by developing a road map, developing hybrid wind/solar/diesel renewable energy projects, and increasing the necessary institutional capacity in the country	NGE
89	Toktogul Rehabilitation Phase 2 Project	Kyrgyz Republic	ADB	Energy efficiency and conservation; energy sector development and institutional reform; large hydropower generation	Project to increase domestic energy supply and international electricity trade, improve asset management and sector planning, and strengthen sector operational performance	NGE
90	Study for a Power Sector Financing Roadmap within CAREC	Regional	ADB	Energy sector development and institutional reform	TA to identify power projects with public–private partnership potential and highlight measures for stimulating private sector interest in the CAREC region's power sector, in addition to reviewing the energy strategy in the CAREC Strategy 2020	NGE

III. Industry, Trade, and Finance

	Project Name	Country	Funder	Project Type	Description	Gender Classification
91	Regional Improvement of Border Services	Mongolia	ADB	Trade and services	Tackling inefficient trade processes by rehabilitating facilities and providing modern equipment to three major border-crossing points, upgrading the Customs Automated Information System, and conducting preparatory work for the establishment of a single-window system for trade-related regulatory requirements	SGE

continued on next page

Industry, Trade, and Finance *continued*

	Project Name	Country	Funder	Project Type	Description	Gender Classification
92	Modernizing Sanitary and Phytosanitary Measures to Facilitate Trade	Regional	ADB	Industry and trade sector development	Supporting the CAREC Common Agenda for the Modernization of Sanitary and Phytosanitary Measures for Trade by (i) creating national bodies in each country and a regional body to lead the modernization process; (ii) developing regulations, procedures, and requirements that are aligned with international standards; and (iii) improving the capability of border agencies to implement these measures at selected common borders	NGE
93	Supporting Economic Corridor Development through Strategic Planning Frameworks	Pakistan	ADB	Industry and trade sector development	Assisting Pakistan to realize the potential of economic corridor development to boost industrial productivity, exports, and job creation and thereby contribute to sustained, increased, and equitable economic growth	NGE
94	Strengthening International Food Safety Standards in Agricultural Value Chains in the CAREC Member Countries	Regional	ADB	Agriculture industry, marketing, and trade	Supporting CAREC countries' implementation of food safety to international standards along agricultural value–chain systems	NGE
95	Implementation of Trade Facilitation Initiatives in CAREC	Regional	ADB	Industry and trade sector development	Supporting the continuation of customs reforms and modernization efforts undertaken by CAREC countries in the framework of the Customs Cooperation Committee	NGE
96	Modernization of Sanitary and Phytosanitary Measures for Food Safety	Turkmenistan	ADB	Agriculture industry, marketing, and trade	Implementing food safety measures in the country and supporting key provisions of the CAREC Transport and Trade Facilitation Strategy 2020 and the CAREC Trade Policy Strategic Action Plan	NGE
97	Regional Upgrades of Sanitary and Phytosanitary Measures for Trade Project	Mongolia	ADB	Trade and services	Supporting the improvement of Sanitary and Phytosanitary measures in Mongolia in compliance with the World Trade Organization Agreement on the Application of such measures.	NGE
98	CAREC Investment Forum	Regional	ADB	Trade and finance	Increasing foreign investors' awareness of opportunities in both mining and non-mining sectors of member economies of the CAREC program, and Mongolia in particular	NGE
99	Building Trade Policy Capacity and Formulating International Trade Policy	Mongolia	ADB	Trade and services	Improving confidence to conduct and conclude mutually beneficial free trade agreements with major trading partners	NGE
100	Supporting Industrial Park Development in the CAREC Region	Regional	ADB	Industry and trade sector development	TA to improve the policy framework for science, industrial and technology parks planning, developing and upgrading in CAREC countries to build the region's industrial productivity and competitiveness	NGE

continued on next page

Industry, Trade, and Finance *continued*

	Project Name	Country	Funder	Project Type	Description	Gender Classification
101	CAREC Working with the Private Sector in Trade Facilitation (Phase 2: CFCFA Strengthening and CPMM)	Regional	ADB	Multimodal logistics	TA to support the implementation of the refined Transport and Trade Facilitation Strategy (TTFS) 2020	NGE

IV. Multisector Projects

	Project Name	Country	Funder	Project Type	Description	Gender Classification
102	Almaty–Bishkek Economic Corridor Support	Regional	ADB	Multiple sectors	TA to support the implementation of the pilot cross-border economic corridor around Almaty and Bishkek within the CAREC program	NGE
103	Enhancing Coordination of the CAREC Program (Supplementary)	Regional	ADB	Multiple sectors	TA to contribute to an expansion in the total international trade of CAREC member countries, as envisaged in CAREC 2020's strategic objective	NGE
104	Promoting Low-Carbon Development in CAREC Program Cities	Regional	ADB	Multiple sectors	TA to support cities in CAREC Program countries to strengthen their capacity to undertake climate actions to further enhance sustainable, inclusive, and prosperous economic development	NGE
105	CAREC: Supporting Capacity Development Needs of CAREC 2020 (Supplementary)	Regional	ADB	Multiple sectors	TA to help meet sector capacity development needs of member countries in implementing CAREC 2020 and also support planning and implementation of their national development plans	NGE
106	Enhancing Coordination of the CAREC Program	Regional	ADB	Multiple sectors	TA to contribute to an expansion in the total international trade of CAREC member countries, as envisaged in CAREC 2020's strategic objective	NGE
107	Enhancing Coordination of the Central Asia Regional Economic Cooperation Program (Supplementary)	Regional	ADB	Multiple sectors	TA to contribute to an expansion in the total international trade of CAREC member countries, as envisaged in CAREC 2020's strategic objective	NGE

ADB = Asian Development Bank, EBRD = European Bank for Reconstruction and Development, ADY = Azerbaijan Railways, CAREC = Central Asia Regional Economic Cooperation, CFCFA = CAREC Federation of Carrier and Forwarder Associations, CIS = Commonwealth of Independent States, CPMM = Corridor Performance Monitoring and Measuring, EGM = effective gender mainstreaming, km = kilometer, kV = kilovolt, GEF = Global Environment Facility, MFF = multitranche financing facility, HPP = hydropower plant, N/A = not applicable, NGE = no gender elements, PFR = Periodic Financing Request, PPTA = project preparatory technical assistance, PRC = People's Republic of China, SGE = some gender elements, TA = technical assistance, TRTA = transaction technical assistance, UNDP = United Nations Development Programme.

Source: ADB. Projects and Tenders. https://www.adb.org/projects (accessed 14 August 2020); EBRD. Project finder. https://www.ebrd.com/project-finder (accessed 14 August 2020); World Bank. Projects and Operations. https://projects.worldbank.org/ (accessed 14 August 2020).

GENDER DESIGN FEATURES OF REVIEWED ADB–FUNDED CAREC TRANSPORT PROJECTS

This table summarizes examples of gender-responsive good practices from ADB-funded transport projects, which were too numerous to include in the main text. The examples are organized by country and by gender indicators that capture commonalities across program design: safety and resilience, economic empowerment, amplifying women's voices, gender-sensitive data and systems, and gender capacity building. There are no projects for the People's Republic of China. Reviewed projects for Pakistan and Turkmenistan do not have gender design features.

#	Safety and Resilience	Economic Empowerment	Amplifying Women's Voices	Gender-Sensitive Data and Systems	Gender Capacity Building
Afghanistan					
1	**Qaisar–Dari Bum Road Project (ADB)**				
	HIV/AIDS prevention and anti–human-trafficking awareness activities	The project will ensure equal pay for equal work among men and women	To ensure that women's needs are dealt with meaningfully, infrastructure subprojects will be selected based on separate consultations with the communities' women, instituted in a culturally appropriate manner	N/A	N/A
2	**Multitranche Financing Facility: Transport Network Development Investment Tranche (ADB)**				
	N/A	N/A	■ Female health action group functional in 50% of project villages ■ Women's involvement through family health action groups	N/A	N/A

	#	Safety and Resilience	Economic Empowerment	Amplifying Women's Voices	Gender-Sensitive Data and Systems	Gender Capacity Building
Azerbaijan		**Railway Sector Development Program (ADB)**				
	1	Improved railway safety from the reconstruction of overpasses and bridges, installation of safety fences and lighting, rest areas with separate toilets for men and women, and a community safety awareness campaign	Advertisements for project-related jobs will include that women are encouraged to apply. ADY will implement a skills development program under the PBL, and ensure 30% participation by women	N/A	N/A	N/A
Georgia		**East–West Highway (Kevi–Ubisa) Section and Improvement Project (ADB)**				
	1	■ Road safety awareness campaign messages reach at least 70% of the targeted total population, out of which at least 40% are women. ■ Installation of road safety facilities that consider the special needs of the elderly, women, and children, such as zebra crossings, safety signs, paved sidewalks, well-lit sheds, paved sidewalks	■ At least 20 Roads Department staff, including all qualifying women staff, have increased knowledge and skills in procurement, project implementation, and project management. ■ Increased number of women employed in technical positions	■ Women's inputs during consultations identified and tracked for incorporation into ensuing decisions and actions ■ Provisions for women's voice and participation in Road Maintenance Sustainability Strategy	■ Project management info system includes gender indicators, sex-disaggregated information monitoring reports on road accidents (sex-disaggregated data) ■ Drafting of action plan to improve gender mainstreaming in Roads Department's policies and programs	■ Engendering road safety programs including the National Road Safety Action Plan and road safety awareness campaign ■ Provisions for women's participation in the Road Maintenance Sustainability Strategy
		North–South Corridor—Kvesheti–Kobi Road (ADB)				
	2	N/A	At least 50 local residents, including 50% of women, gained knowledge and skills from tourism-related job and business trainings.	N/A	Disaggregate data on parties involved in road accidents	Ensure participation of female staff in technical trainings
		CAREC Corridors 2, 3, and 5 (Obigarm–Nurobod) Road Project (ADB)				
	3	N/A	Training of selected Ministry of Transport and Government Automobile Road Establishment staff (50% of whom will be women) on tunnel operation and management, including climate change and disaster risk management	N/A	N/A	N/A

#	Safety and Resilience	Economic Empowerment	Amplifying Women's Voices	Gender-Sensitive Data and Systems	Gender Capacity Building
Kazakhstan					
1	**CAREC Corridors 1 and 6 Connector (Aktobe–Makat) Reconstruction Project (ADB)**				
	Gender-sensitive road safety features will be included in designated parts of the project route, including lighting, roadside rest areas with separate toilets for men and women, bus stops, and sidewalks.	Advertisements for project-related jobs will include a sentence to the effect that women are encouraged to apply.	The participation plan in the Land Acquisition and Resettlement Plan includes strategies to ensure that women's voices are heard.	Progress reports with socioeconomic data disaggregated by sex will provide periodic updates on the effects of land acquisition and relocation on women. Indicators to be used for reporting include (i) sex-disaggregated information on employment and pay, and (ii) sex-disaggregated information on the number and type of training provided. The Land Acquisition Resettlement Plan monitoring report will include sex-disaggregated data on the involvement of affected people.	N/A
Kyrgyz Republic					
1	**CAREC Corridors 1 and 3 Connector Road Project**				
	Carry out HIV/AIDS, illicit drug, and human trafficking prevention and awareness programs in workers' campsites; road safety and protection of drivers, passengers, pedestrians, and livestock, including sidewalks, footpaths, taxi/bus stops and stations, street lighting; designation of safe sites for seasonal vending and roadside services, drinking water and toilet facilities, lay-bys, pull-offs, and rest areas for the comfort of travelers	**Phase 2:** At least 10% of the employed office staff and project construction workers are women.	**Phase 2:** ■ Women's organizations part of design workshop ■ Tripartite commission including civil society organizations	■ During construction phase, monitoring to include employment in project construction with attention to national origin, gender, position/skill level ■ Design based on social summary matrix supporting women's participation in design review workshops, project consultations, and the mitigation of project-associated social risks for women, as well as attention to women's employment in project construction and measures encouraging women's opportunities in road-related enterprise development	**Phase 2:** ■ Women staff of the Ministry of Transport and Roads will be included in relevant capacity-building activities

Mongolia

Phase 2 note under Gender-Sensitive Data and Systems:

Phase 2: Additional Financing
- Project monitoring will include the regular collection of sex-disaggregated data and report on gender-relevant achievements on other issues such as inclusive employment and data on accident incidence by gender, age, residence, and type.

#	Safety and Resilience	Economic Empowerment	Amplifying Women's Voices	Gender-Sensitive Data and Systems	Gender Capacity Building
1	**Regional Road Development and Maintenance Project (ADB)**				
	▪ Prevent negative impacts such as HIV/AIDS, sexually transmitted infections, sexual harassment, and trafficking in persons, especially to women; 250 people, of which at least 50% were women, participated in training and awareness campaign activities ▪ Conduct road safety training for residents with participation of women; 800 residents along the project road (at least 50% women) trained and reported on the improved awareness on road safety and related activities as a result of the training ▪ Conduct safety driving training to drivers sensitizing risky male drivers; 400 drivers (especially men) trained on safety driving	▪ Conduct civil works with participation of women; at least 15% women employed in unskilled construction works under the project and guaranteed equal pay for equal work, supplied with safety equipment, toilet, and changing rooms ▪ Support local development initiatives; 400 people, of which at least 50% were women, participated in training on small businesses and income-generation methods alongside the corridor to be organized by local nongovernment organizations	Ensure thorough public consultation on construction activities; Women comprised at least 40% of participants to community and household consultation meetings on project construction activities	N/A	At least 30 staff, including at least 50% of whom were women, who attended training report improved skills on road asset management
2	**MFF: Western Regional Road Corridor Development Program Tranche 2 (ADB)**				
	N/A	▪ At least 30% of construction labor to be hired locally, specially focusing on local herders, ethnic minority communities, and the poor and vulnerable. Of the 30% construction jobs, 20% to be provided to local women.	N/A	N/A	N/A

Tajikistan

#	Safety and Resilience	Economic Empowerment	Amplifying Women's Voices	Gender-Sensitive Data and Systems	Gender Capacity Building
		■ Local population focusing on women, herders, ethnic minorities, and households headed by disabled women to engage in small enterprises to be set up along the road. At least 20% of these will be women.			
1	**CAREC Corridors 2, 5, and 6 (Dushanbe–Kurgonteppa) Road Project Additional Financing (ADB)**				
	Project design will address some of the factors that inhibit female mobility by increasing safety features (road signs and street lighting), enhancing connectivity of villages (pedestrian crossings and livestock underpasses), constructing bus stops, improving rest areas and road bazaars, and promoting confidence in the new road configuration through road safety awareness training and workshops	N/A	N/A	N/A	N/A
2	**Preparing CAREC Corridors 2, 3, and 5 (Obigarm–Nurobod) Road Project (ADB)**				
	N/A	N/A	N/A	Feasibility study on ensuing project prepared. This output will include preparing project cost estimates, and preparing safeguards documentation for the environmental and social aspects of the project consistent with ADB's Safeguards Policy Statement 2009.	Include women staff in technical trainings— at least 20 staff including 50% women have increased knowledge and skills on operation and maintenance of tunnels, including climate change disaster risk management

Uzbekistan

#	Safety and Resilience	Economic Empowerment	Amplifying Women's Voices	Gender-Sensitive Data and Systems	Gender Capacity Building
1	**CAREC Corridor 2 (Pap–Namangan–Andijan) Railway Electrification Project (ADB)**				
	■ (i) Assessing the existing and anticipated safety situation to the general public, (ii) supporting the development of practical countermeasures, and (iii) training staff to plan future railway developments in the safest manner ■ The special safety needs of women and children will be considered in the safety action plan that the project will develop	N/A	N/A	N/A	O'zbekiston Temir Yo'llari staff, including all women technical staff, will be trained on safe railway operations
2	**Railway Efficiency Improvement Project**				
	N/A	N/A	■ Perceptions of women in technical positions as input into long-term development strategy ■ Female employees' feedback into draft design of locomotive depot upgrade ■ Female employees' review and provide feedback into long-term development strategy		

ADB = Asian Development Bank, ADY = Azerbaijan Railways, CAREC = Central Asia Regional Economic Cooperation, PBL = policy-based lending, MFF = multitranche financing facility, N/A = not applicable.

Source: ADB. Projects and Tenders. https://www.adb.org/projects (accessed 14 August 2020).

KEY FINDINGS FROM COUNTRY RESEARCH MISSIONS TO AZERBAIJAN, KAZAKHSTAN, AND UZBEKISTAN

The decision to field missions in these countries was based on the fact that Central Asia Regional Economic Cooperation (CAREC) investment in these countries accounts for around 70% of total development programming. A visit to Afghanistan had also been planned but did not take place because of security concerns.

The gender consultant responsible for the formulation of the CAREC Gender Assessment and Strategy held meetings and interviews with relevant CAREC stakeholders. Key findings and issues discussed during these meetings are summarized below.

I. AZERBAIJAN

A. Key Findings and Issues Discussed

1. **World Bank**

   - World Bank is one of the key CAREC development partners. In the meeting, most of the discussion was about the World Bank portfolio in Azerbaijan related to CAREC and to gender. It was appreciated that Asian Development Bank (ADB) was creating the most opportunities in its transport projects for gender integration.
   - World Bank's work on rural infrastructure has focused on women's participation and economic empowerment. Specifically, the creation of community interest groups has prioritized women and youth groups for developing income-generation initiatives under their work program on rural infrastructure.
   - Women's community saving groups have also been introduced in projects. These saving groups pool their savings and go through a cycle of one member getting the pooled amount every month. Women have opened businesses such as bakeries and school canteens with this money.
   - Missing girls in the South Caucuses and the gender wage gap were highlighted as key concerns in the country.

2. **Project Officer for the Power Distribution Enhancement Investment Program in Azerbaijan, ADB**[1]

- The discussion highlighted two crucial gaps in meaningfully integrating gender in energy distribution projects:
  (i) **Limited female electrical and mechanical engineers.** As the project has to deliver on results, it can train available women engineers, but it cannot do much about increasing the number of available female engineers, which is at the heart of the issue.
  (ii) **Limited engagement with country-level discussions and priority setting on gender.** Educational choices are a combination of expected gender roles, availability of opportunities, and several cultural and policy factors. To enhance science, technology, engineering, and mathematics (STEM) education for women, more concentrated multisector intervention is needed, encompassing several interrelated issues and using a holistic approach.
- Women's participation in governing boards can be considered during loan negotiations. This is impactful as it brings in the female perspective and these women function as role models for young girls wanting to pursue careers in so-called nontraditional fields like energy.

3. **Azerbaijan's Women Entrepreneurs Association**

- Economic empowerment was highlighted as a potential area for further cooperation. Given the current legislative and operating landscape for civil society organizations (CSOs) in Azerbaijan, they have set up sister private companies to continue their work.
- Different CSOs are unanimous in the need for a more enabling framework of operations for CSOs in Azerbaijan.
- Business Women Association(s) (BWAs) in Azerbaijan have strong regional linkages with CAREC countries and Turkey. There is a willingness to build on these linkages and be part of a regional network of women business associations. BWAs are membership-driven organizations, which reflects the potential for more dynamism in the micro, small, and medium-sized enterprises (MSMEs) sector in Azerbaijan. For meaningful regional linkages for Azeri women, the following readiness steps were suggested:
  (i)   gender integration frameworks in banks and insurance companies to improve access to finance for women in business,
  (ii) emphasis on training in product development and value-chain promotion,
  (iii) alignment of legal and policy frameworks to enhance entrepreneurship rights for women, and
  (iv) sex-disaggregated data to ensure data-driven policy.

4. **ADB and CAREC Country-Based Staff**

- The discussion identified the need to increase women's participation in STEM education, reduce the gender wage gaps, and strengthen participation of women in sectors such as energy and transport.

---

[1] ADB. 2015. *Azerbaijan: Power Distribution Enhancement Investment Program.* Manila. https://www.adb.org/projects/42401-014/main.

- Some identified opportunities for gender mainstreaming were the following:
  (i) **Tourism.** The government of Azerbaijan is promoting tourism development by ensuring infrastructure availability for tourists, and by facilitating the e-visa. Women are participating as staff in tourist agencies and in the hospitality industry. These can be built on and other areas can be explored, especially for nonbusiness tourists. Avenues for women's participation in partnership with the recently established State Tourism Agency Azerbaijan can be explored.
  (ii) **Digital access for women.** Women lag behind in information and communication technology (ICT). Partnership with government on taking forward the gender strategy in this direction may be explored.

B. Recommendations

1. Integrate lessons learned from power distribution project into the assessment.
2. Increase the engagement of BWAs in the implementation of the CAREC gender strategy.

II. KAZAKHSTAN

A. Key Findings and Issues Discussed

1. Sustainable Development Goals Focal Point

- Gender integration is a priority on the policy agenda for the country. Two possible opportunities for collaboration are
  (i) policy dialogue and knowledge sharing, and
  (ii) generating sex-disaggregated data.
- As part of the Sustainable Development Goals prioritization, the government has prioritized 297 targets. For the Voluntary National Review, the department worked with the Committee on Statistics, on a specific chapter on gender-disaggregated indicators.
- Women in Business, as part of a multicountry program by the European Bank for Reconstruction and Development (EBRD), was highlighted as a good practice to encourage women entrepreneurs. Women participate in some 45% of MSMEs in Kazakhstan. Financed by the Government of Kazakhstan, the Entrepreneurship Development Fund has partnered with EBRD to provide access to finance and business development and leadership trainings. The loans are administered through commercial banks in the country.
- Initiatives for encouraging women in STEM include a scholarship program financing studies abroad.
- Issues raised for continued efforts were the gender pay gap, the gender gap in decision-making and management positions in quasi-state bodies and multinationals, and instances of domestic violence, more so in the regions.

2. **Business Women Association**

- The following areas were highlighted as having potential for further collaboration with CAREC in gender mainstreaming at a regional level by connecting businesswomen across the 11 countries:
  (i) establishment of an online multilingual portal using English and other national languages. Among the modules for the portal would be information available in the region, online training in different skills, business ethics, and law for different countries in CAREC; and
  (ii) a possible regional network of BWAs.
- Established in 1996, the Business Women Association is the largest nongovernment organization in Kazakhstan. They are also a partner in EBRD's Women in Business program in Kazakhstan. They believe that there is a large market that needs to be serviced specifically by providing financial access and training in business skills for women.
- It operates a three-tiered system, with senior businesswomen, some of them founders of the organization, at the first tier. These are followed by the middle tier of women aged 35–60. This tier forms the majority of the membership. The third tier is for young entrepreneurs, who are mostly under 35.
- The Business Women Association has linkages with BWAs in Mongolia, Afghanistan, Uzbekistan, the United Arab Emirates, and the Russian Federation.

In terms of trends, most women in business are working through small and medium-sized enterprises in Kazakhstan. Generally, women do not invest outside Kazakhstan. Areas of business that bring together Kazakh business strengths and areas where women are or can easily work, as discussed, included
  (i) medical tourism;
  (ii) educational exchange, emphasizing orthodontia services, which are in demand in the region;
  (iii) advanced cosmetology; and
  (iv) tourism and hospitality.

3. **The World Bank**

- In the meeting, most of the discussions were on the project-level implementation of World Bank Gender Strategy, 2016. Broadly, this strategy integrates at analysis, design, and monitoring and evaluation stages. It carries forward the element of gender information project development through background assessments. It adds gender tagging across the results chain for the project. This enables better monitoring of the project gender results to achieve the project development objective.

4. **Chamber of Commerce of Kazakhstan**

- ADB is partnering with chambers of commerce to train women in the region in business development through a series of 2-day workshops. The course content concentrates on business development and access to finance. Banks operating at the local level are also invited to talk about their financial products for MSMEs. Women have a 77% higher rate of rejection of finance from formal banking institutions. The detailed information on requirements and documentation is to help reduce the gender gap in access to finance. Bookkeeping, business plans, and taxation laws and paperwork are also part of the sessions.

- Fintech and digitization are potential areas to create economic opportunities for women. For example, through initiatives such as the government-to-people (G2P) payment system like Kaspi Bank, which is recognized to be an opportunity for social security and gender mainstreaming. This demonstrates a certain level of penetration and outreach beyond bigger cities, as well.
- An innovative project in the soft pipeline is to support women in housing mortgage.

5. ADB and CAREC Country-Based Staff

- There is limited participation of women in the transport, energy, and trade sectors. Men also predominate in technical and managerial jobs in these sectors, in both at government and private agencies.
- There is a scope for work in this regard by developing more projects with gender elements and ensuring results for mainstreaming gender into the sector, and not just the project, are emphasized.

B. Recommendations

1. Extract best practices and lessons learned from projects implemented in Kazakhstan in gender mainstreaming.
2. Increase engagement of BWAs in the implementation of the CAREC gender strategy.

III. UZBEKISTAN

A. Key Findings and Issues Discussed

1. CAREC Country-Based Staff

- The meeting acknowledged Uzbekistan's continued commitment to gender equality and women's empowerment, which has been reinvigorated with the inclusion of women in prominent parliamentary positions.
- It was noted that ADB's Uzbekistan Resident Mission is well integrated with the country's CSOs, which work across a diverse set of sectors and areas. Leveraging this integration for CAREC remains a key challenge.
- During the meeting, it was mentioned that the BWA of Uzbekistan Tadbikor Ayol has partnered with ADB since 2006. BWA membership comes mostly from small and medium-sized enterprises. This BWA has interacted with women entrepreneurs from other countries within the region and considers it an important interaction that merits regular meetings.
- Ensuring safe border crossings for women among CAREC countries was identified as a key issue to be addressed.
- Additional mechanisms could be explored by CAREC to mainstream gender into its operations. For example, increased participation of women in CAREC activities should be encouraged through the nomination of female experts.
- It was noted that in most CAREC projects related to transport, energy, and trade, women participate as beneficiaries. However, their level of participation differs from project to project.

- Opportunities for CAREC to build on for gender integration under CAREC 2030:
    (i)   girls in STEM (an example of recently started TechGirls giving scholarships for STEM education was cited),
    (ii) ICT as a cross-cutting theme, and
    (iii) opportunities stemming from regional tourism projects.

2. Project Officer for the Small Business and Entrepreneurship Development Project in Uzbekistan[2]

- This project was highlighted as a good practice of gender mainstreaming. The project was formulated to address the need to improve the ability of small businesses, including those of women, to operate, expand, access finance, and benefit from economic opportunities. Some of the key elements in the success of interventions were as follows:
    (i)   Make sure that money is used for the project's beneficiaries.
    (ii) Formulation of the Gender Action Plan, including activities and indicators, to ensure female board members and women in management positions across bank operations. Currently, 50% of employees of the participating commercial banks are women.
    (iii) An overarching partnership framework involving local administration, civil society specifically, BWAs, participating commercial banks, and development partners was regarded as enhancing effectiveness of the project.

3. Project Officer for the Surkhandarya Regional Road Project in Uzbekistan[3]

- The multidisciplinary nature of meaningful gender integration was highlighted. The following areas of gender integration were emphasized:
    (i)   synergies with MSME projects to support women-led business in road catchment area,
    (ii) avenues for influencing hiring practices of the Uzbek Agency for Automobile and River Agency, and
    (iii) development of menu of activities for women-run businesses along CAREC corridors as a standard for all corridor projects.

- Some of the recommendations raised during the meeting were
    (i)   to deconstruct the default "male" in project design for transport and energy;
    (ii) to include a combination of qualitative and quantitative gender indicators for ADB-designed projects;
    (iii) to mainstream gender in all sectors, but specifically in agriculture and textiles, given the impact of rural migration on agricultural labor and the emphasis on cotton as an export and the value chain of fruit exports; and
    (iv) to support the gathering of sex-disaggregated data, specifically at the district level.

[2]   ADB. 2019. *Uzbekistan: Small Business and Entrepreneurship Development Project.* Manila. https://www.adb.org/sites/default/files/evaluation-document/514581/files/pvr-625.pdf.
[3]   ADB. 2019. *Uzbekistan: Preparing the Surkhandarya Regional Road Project.* Manila. adb.org/projects/53312-002/main#project-pds-collapse.

B. Recommendations

1. Integrate lessons learned from both the Small Business and Entrepreneurship Development Project and the Surkhandarya Regional Road Project in the assessment.
2. Increase the engagement of BWAs for the implementation of the CAREC gender strategy.